FROM OP
TO HOPE

FROM OPTIMISM
TO HOPE

Thoughts for the day

JONATHAN SACKS

continuum

Continuum

The Tower Building
11 York Road
London SE1 7NX

15 East 26th Street
New York
NY 10010

www.continuumbooks.com

© Jonathan Sacks 2004

First published 2004

British Library Cataloguing-in-Publication Data
A catalogue record for this book is available from the British Library.

ISBN 08264 74810

'September 1, 1939' by W. H. Auden reproduced courtesy of Faber and Faber Ltd.

Designed and typeset by Benn Linfield
Printed and bound by MPG Books Limited, Bodmin, UK

To Trevor, Daniela, Sabrina,
Tania and Jason
Cherished friends

Contents

Introduction

It is, to be honest, one of the odder features of British life. There you are, at about ten to eight in the morning, spreading the marmalade, or stuck in a traffic jam, getting ready to face another day, when on the radio, in the midst of news of the latest earthquake or political row or terrorist attack, there comes an innocent and indecently cheerful voice *giving you a sermon*. It's probably enough to make you want to give up there and then.

But I'm a fan of *Thought for the Day*, that non-commercial break in the middle of BBC Radio 4's morning news programme, *Today*. I always loved the *Today* programme, from those distant days when Jack de Manio used to be the presenter, generously spreading confusion by getting the time wrong, making a significant slice of the nation think either that they should be back in bed or that they were desperately late for their first appointment of the day. If he could get it wrong, why shouldn't we? It was a tutorial in keeping a sense of proportion.

And keeping a sense of proportion is what *Thought for the Day* is about. I suppose it is a residue from the days in which the BBC, still guarding its Reithian legacy, used to see itself as the conscience of the nation, making sure that there was an act of daily worship on prime time radio every day and shutting down on Sunday evenings (once upon a time there was no morning television) so that people could have no excuse for missing church.

Hence *Thought for the Day*, a religious reflection on some news item from the previous twenty-four hours, to remind us that as well as news, there is also (why not coin a word for it?) *olds*: the wisdom of the past, an echo of eternity, a way of stepping back from the pace and thrust of now and seeing events from a more distant perspective – not a bad thing to do once in a while.

There is, after all, that little matter of *trying to make sense* of what is going on out there in the world, of seeing history as more than Joseph Heller, author of *Catch-22*, put it: 'a trash bag of random coincidences blown open by the wind'. *Homo sapiens* is the meaning-seeking animal, which is why there is the phenomenon we call religion – humanity's greatest collective attempt to find meaning in this brief, tempestuous, often pain-filled span of days we call life.

Hegel, that otherwise impenetrable philosopher, once said that modern man reads newspapers as a substitute for prayer. If so, it is a pretty poor substitute, because prayer did at least embody the faith that somehow, from a heavenly perspective at least, it *did* make sense, whereas the media have no such commitment. An exclusive diet of news is hardly likely to convince us that there is some script of which we are a part, a plot to whose unfolding we are the witnesses, some narrative that allows us to understand what is happening and why.

Which is why I have so enjoyed doing *Thought for the Day* for many years now. It is a way of saying, 'Hang on guys, let's pause, stop and think what this means.' What would our ancestors make of it? What, looking back with hindsight, will our grandchildren think about it? And how does it fit within that cosmic drama into which we have been thrust, like it or not, for as along as we are around to care.

I believe – in fact it is one of the Bible's greatest contributions to civilization, utterly revolutionary in its day – that time *is* a narrative; that history is an ongoing dialogue between us, our baser instincts and our highest ideals; that it tells a story if we try hard enough to decode it. Nor is it accidental that we tell stories, of which the most important are about where we have come from, where we are going to, and why. Without that, life has no meaning.

Of course, many in this unprecedentedly secular age believe just that, that life has no meaning and that news – the world's endlessly turning ferris wheel, a global London Eye – is all there is. That view is certainly coherent. It is ancient as well as modern (the Greek philosopher Epicurus thought so too, and warned us against having hopes because they would always end in disillusion). But it strikes me as being *tone-deaf*. There is music beneath the noise, meaning beneath the surface, but we have to pause to hear it. Religion is more than a system of beliefs. It is an act of focused listening – to the script of which we are the heroes and, with God, the co-authors.

That, after all, is what Tolstoy thought, and kept saying through perhaps the greatest novel ever written, *War and Peace*. The people in the thick of the battle, he believed, never knew what was actually going on. That needed the eye of a novelist. Later he came to the conclusion that it needed the eye of faith, and promptly gave up writing novels and dedicated himself to good works and devotional tracts. One of the good things about *Thought for the Day* is that it is decidedly shorter than *War and Peace*. (It takes two minutes, forty-five seconds. It used to take three minutes, but the BBC decided to shorten it on the grounds that *no one can concentrate for three minutes any more*. Now that's worth a *Thought*.)

The years from which these reflections are taken (from 1995 to the first day of 2004) have been unsettling and disturbing. The year 2000 saw the collapse of the Peace Process in the Middle East and a campaign of suicide bombings that must rank as one of the most destructive and self-destructive in the history of that troubled place. A year later came 9/11, an act of calculated outrage which brought down more than the Twin Towers of New York. It ended the era of cautious optimism that accompanied the end of the Cold War, the fall of the Berlin Wall, the collapse of apartheid in

South Africa, and – in the West at least – the longest economic boom in living memory.

Since then there have been the wars in Afghanistan and Iraq and the toppling of the Taleban and Saddam Hussein – successful in one sense, yet uneasy victories, if indeed victories they prove to be. We have learned that it is easy to defeat tyrants but much harder to construct free societies with the self-restraints and civilities they require. The 'new world order' looks suspiciously like the old world disorder, described by the Bible as the state of humanity before the Flood, and memorably characterized by Hobbes in *The Leviathan* as a war of 'every man against every man' in which there is 'continual fear and danger of violent death; and the life of man solitary, poor, nasty, brutish and short'.

Hobbes was writing in the 1640s and 1650s against the background of the wars of religion that had thrown Europe into turmoil for a century. Perhaps that is our greatest fear as we face the twenty-first century: that we face another era of wars of religion (or as Samuel Huntington calls them, 'clashes of civilizations'), only this time with weapons of far greater powers of destruction. In fact one of the things 9/11 did was to remind us how even the most innocent objects can be turned to murderous ends. Before then, how many of us thought of jumbo jets, skyscrapers and box-cutters as lethal weapons capable of bringing death to thousands? If we have learned anything from that day it is that evil exists not in objects in the external world but in the human mind and its capacity for hate. Freud was right: civilization is sustained in the *psyche*, the word that means 'the soul', and in its eternal battle between what he called *eros* and *thanatos*, the 'pleasure principle' and the 'death instinct'. Indeed the words that echo most powerfully from 9/11 were first written sixty-two years earlier by W. H. Auden (in his poem 'September 1, 1939'):

The unmentionable odour of death
Offends the September night ...
All I have is a voice
To undo the folded lie,
The romantic lie in the brain
Of the sensual man-in-the-street
And the lie of Authority
Whose buildings grope the sky:
There is no such thing as the State
And no one exists alone ...
We must love one another or die.

In the closing lines of that poem Auden defines his duty as a poet, which surely serves for all of us (I know it does for me): 'May I, composed like them / Of Eros and of dust, / Beleaguered by the same / Negation and despair, / Show an affirming flame.'

That is what I tried to do in so many of these *Thoughts* – to articulate a hope, 'show an affirming flame'. There is nothing inevitable or logical about hope. There are cultures in which it does not exist. There is no reason – based on scientific law or historical experience – to believe that tomorrow will be better than today (my wife Elaine used to have a poster on the wall that read, 'They said "Cheer up – things could be worse." So I cheered up ... and sure enough, things got worse.'). Hope is, as sociologist Peter Berger called it, a *signal of transcendence* – something that speaks to us from beyond where we are. If I were to define the task I set myself in the past four years, it was to be an agent of hope.

Hope is ultimately a religious emotion. It is born in the conviction that we are more than a blind concatenation of 'selfish genes'. That may be one way of describing what we are, but it is not *all* we are, and to believe otherwise is to be deaf to the music of life itself. Philosophers, ancient and modern, have sometimes spoken as if it

FROM OPTIMISM TO HOPE

were an act of intellectual courage to believe that there is no meaning to human existence, that we are cosmic dust in a universe blind to our hopes, indifferent to our prayers. I for one, however, have never been sure why nihilism is a more courageous stance than faith – faith that the very existence of the universe and the emergence of the one being thus far discovered capable of asking 'Why?' testify, in their sheer improbability, to some real (if doubtless obscure) purpose.

We are here, I believe, because someone wanted us to be; who created us in love; who knows our fears, hears our cries, and believes in us more than we believe in ourselves, lifting us when we fall, giving us strength when strength fails, who forgives our mistakes so long as we acknowledge that they were mistakes; who holds us in his everlasting arms and who, though others may reject us, never does. And if all that should prove untrue, then I would rather be accused of taking the risk of believing the best about existence than of having taken refuge in the safety of believing the worst.

And if all this is too metaphysical, let me put it another way. A while back our office leased a car with a satellite navigation system. This is a brilliant device. You key in your destination, and a polite voice and a map tell you where to go. Jewish drivers always know better – a short cut here, a detour there ('What does the computer know? I grew up here'). What fascinates me is the way the device responds. It pauses for a moment to take in the fact that its instr-uctions have been ignored. It then flashes up a signal, 'Recalculating the route', and – lo and behold – it works out a new route based on your current position. To this electronic miracle of persistence, I owe one of the great lessons of life: that *wherever you are and wherever you wish to be, there's a route between here and there.* If that isn't grounds for hope, I don't know what is. Which is what, one way or another, I've tried to say in most of these *Thoughts*.

Yet sometimes we have to create hope. It is not simply there to be plucked like fruit from a tree someone else has planted. And here I must be candid about the deepest fear that has haunted me these past three years and robbed me of sleep through many restless nights.

The twenty-first century has witnessed – in many parts of the world, if not in Britain – a revival of religion. The reasons are complex, but at least part of the story is simply told. In an age of change we seek refuge in the things that do not change. At times of confusion we thirst for certainty. The terms of politics have changed. If the twentieth century was the *age of ideology*, the twenty-first will be seen as the *age of identity* in which people disillusioned with politics turned to the most fundamental questions of all: 'Why am I here?' and 'Who am I?'

These are questions that cannot be answered by politics or economics, which tell us what and how, but not why or who. The search for meaning and identity always ends in religion. But in the very act of providing a solution, it also creates a problem. Religion binds people together in a network of belonging. The word itself comes from a Latin root meaning 'to bind'. It turns 'I' into 'we'. It shapes disparate selves into a community. But 'we' is always defined by contrast with a 'they' – the ones who are *not like us*, whose ideals, values, rituals and narratives are different from ours. Religion divides as it unites. 'If only,' we say, 'the world were like us – we who value love and peace, forgiveness and brotherhood.' But the world is *not* like us, nor will it be until the end of days. Religion has not done well in valuing diversity.

In the past, that mattered less than it does today. For most of history, many people have lived in close proximity to those with whom they shared a culture and a way of life. This has changed. Through global communications, ease of travel, migration and the fragmentation of culture, we now live in the continuous, conscious presence of difference. That, for many people, is profoundly threatening.

The result is fundamentalism, specifically the use of violence to impose our vision on others. The results can be traced in conflict zones throughout the world. We live in an age in which, in the words of Jonathan Swift, 'we have just enough religion to make us hate one another but not enough to make us love one another'.

This may seem a long way from *Thought for the Day*, but strangely it is not. *Thought* asks one thing from its contributors that is all too rare today. It invites each of us, whatever our faith, to talk to people who are not of our faith. It asks us to broadcast, not narrowcast. It forces us to speak inclusively, respecting the diversity of those listening. It is a standing invitation to generosity of spirit. It reminds us that though our faiths are many, our fate is one.

And, being a rabbi, I could not end without illustrating the point with a story. This one is true. In late 1990, Dr George Carey had been elected but not yet taken up office as Archbishop of Canterbury. I had been elected, but not yet taken up office, as Chief Rabbi. Somehow, someone discovered that we were both passionate Arsenal supporters. He got in touch with both of us and asked whether we would like our first ecumenical gathering to take place in his box in Highbury Stadium – a midweek match for obvious religious reasons. We both replied enthusiastically that we would.

The great day arrived. It was little less than heaven itself. We arrived at the box and were taken down to meet the players. We went out, underneath the floodlights, onto the sacred turf itself to present a cheque to charity. The loudspeakers announced our presence. You could hear the buzz go around the ground. Whichever way one chose in the theological wager, that night Arsenal had friends in high places. They could not possibly lose.

A nachtiger tog, as my grandmother would say: Would that it were so. That night Arsenal went down to their worst home defeat in sixty-three years. They lost 6–2 to Manchester United. The Archbishop was beside himself in agony.

The next day one of the national newspapers ran the story and concluded that if, between them, the prayers of the Archbishop of Canterbury and the Chief Rabbi could not bring about a win for Arsenal, did this not finally prove that *God does not exist*? The next day I wrote back, saying: On the contrary, what it proves is that God exists. It's just that *He supports Manchester United!*

Which is a way of saying that if only we remembered that, yes, God is on our side, but He is also on the other side, we might stand a chance of realizing that, under the eye of heaven we are all on the same side, the side of humanity. The game is more important than the teams, and what is at stake implicates us all. We must, as Auden said, love one another or die.

THE WISDOM TO DECIDE

31 January 2003

Nothing is harder, and few things more fateful, than knowing when to fight a war. In ancient times, the people of God heard the voice of God. They had prophets and oracles. The book of Ecclesiastes, in words that were true then and true now, said that there is a time for war and a time for peace. The difference is that then people were sure which was which. Today we see as through a glass darkly. Anyone today who tells you that he hears the voice of God telling him to kill is a liar and a fraud. If we knew the future, we could act with certainty. But to be human is to live with uncertainty and yet still have the courage and the wisdom to decide.

Many people, with great courage, have said: to wage war against Iraq is wrong. There will be casualties and among them will be the innocent. We have too little knowledge to be sure exactly what weapons Saddam Hussein has and how and against whom he intends to use them. How can a mere possibility override the certainty of the suffering and death war will cause? That is a serious argument, and I respect it from the depths of my soul.

But I also hear, from those same depths, another voice. A voice that says: the tragedy and devastation of 11 September was only a beginning, the first flash of lightning in a storm that threatens to engulf the world. We face an age of global terror and rogue states, driven by none of the conventions of war as we have known it, ruthless in their contempt for life, capable if not checked of holding a sword of Damocles over all of us, if not now then in the lifetimes of our children. And may we – we who hold the future in trust for them – allow that to happen, unhalted, unchecked?

Twelve years ago, during the Gulf War, I sat with my wife and children in our sealed rooms in Jerusalem as 39 times SCUD missiles rained down on city streets and we never knew whether the next one would contain chemical or biological weapons. And as I looked at our eight-year-old daughter wearing her gas mask I thought, 'This is not a world to give her or any child.' Somehow we have to say, 'Stop.'

And so I pray, 'Dear God, spare us from the need for war; but if it must be, then give our leaders the wisdom, and those who fight, the skill, to minimize the suffering and loss of life; and let this be the beginning of the end of a reign of terror so that we may find another way.'

COMMUNITY

6 March 2000

A couple of years ago, a friend of mine was mugged. He was going home one night from the synagogue when a group of youths attacked him, hit him and threw him to the ground. He struggled home, hurt not just physically but psychologically as well.

Then something strange and rather moving took place. When he was missing next morning at the synagogue, people noticed and phoned up. They found out what had happened; and from then on there was a constant stream of well-wishers, some bringing him food, others just their company, until he recovered. And when the police came round a few days later to take a statement, he said: 'I know this is going to sound strange, but I almost want to thank my attackers. They showed me the friends I never knew I had.'

It's an extreme example, I suppose, but it tells us what community is at its best. It's where we are there for other people and they are there for us; not because of the state or the market; not because of a relationship of power or exchange; but just because we're bound by the bonds of mutual belonging. It's where the 'We' takes precedence over the 'I'.

In the last few weeks we've had some important messages about community. There was the Chancellor of the Exchequer's call for a new civic patriotism. And last Thursday the Prime Minister launched a major conference on communities and the voluntary sector. It was the right message at the right time. According to research published today, a third of us don't know our next-door neighbours; and more people than ever are living alone. And yet, in the book of Genesis only one thing is called 'not good'. It's not good for man to be alone. And today we need to strengthen the fabric of togetherness out of which a society is made.

In Judaism we call a house of prayer a *bet knesset*, meaning, the home of the community; and religions, at their best, are community-building institutions. As a rabbi I see more than my share of people going through crisis; and time and again I'm touched by the sight of people rallying round, giving help and comfort and support and strength. A community is where we create the things you can't buy in a shop or be given by act of Parliament: friendship; loyalty; generosity; and trust – the things that only exist in virtue of being shared.

We need communities to soften the rough edges of an abrasive world. Too often society is a place of strangers where what we need is an extended family of friends. So if you were to ask me what a community is, I'd say it's the place where they know who you are, and where they miss you if you're not there. Community is society with a human face – the place where we know we're not alone.

WRITING IN THE BOOK OF LIFE

13 September 1996

Tomorrow and the day after will be Rosh Hashanah, the Jewish New Year. And if I were to try and define what these days are about, I'd say they were a Jewish equivalent of *Thought for the Day*, or better still, a Thought for the Year, a reflective pause in the rush of daily events. On Rosh Hashanah we stop thinking about the news headlines, and think about life itself, and how we've used ours. We count our blessings, and enumerate our faults. We think of the times we could have helped others but didn't. We apologize to God and ask Him to forgive us. And we pray to be written in the book of life. It's a bit like the two files I keep on my desk. One is very large, and marked 'urgent'. The other is thin and a bit neglected. It's marked 'important'. Rosh Hashanah is when we ignore the urgent and concentrate on the important: life as the most precious gift of God.

Which is why, this year, I'll be thinking of two friends who died in the course of the past twelve months, but who wrote distinguished chapters in the book of life. The first was the late Prime Minister of Israel, Yitzhak Rabin. Rabin was one of Israel's military heroes, a former Chief of Staff. But towards the end of his life, as the pain and grief of war mounted, he changed direction. He shook hands with his former enemies, and began the long tough road to peace in the Middle East. He took great risks, and in the end he was assassinated. Weeks before he died, we shared our views on the situation. I spoke of the rising tensions in Israel. But he, like the giant he was, was determined to press ahead. He couldn't bear, he said, to see so many bereaved parents and children, so many people killed in the course of conflict. He taught us courage in pursuit of life.

The other was the late Hugo Gryn, broadcaster and rabbi of the West London synagogue. Hugo and I were at opposite ends of the religious spectrum, but we were friends. What was remarkable about him was that as a child he'd lived through the hell of Auschwitz. Who would have blamed him if he'd spent the rest of his life traumatized and haunted? But he didn't. Instead he dedicated his career to caring for others and working for better understanding between faiths. Incredibly, he never lost his sense of humour, or his trust in humanity, or his gift of hope. He taught us courage in the affirmation of life.

For me, these two friends showed what's really important: to write other people in the book of life.

A GATEWAY OF HOPE

12 June 2000

The death, over the weekend, of the Syrian president, Hafez al-Assad, has thrown the political map of the Middle East into confusion; and we surely wish his successor well in the long search for a formula that will allow all peoples in that much-afflicted region to live together in peace.

At moments like this I can't help thinking in very personal terms, because in the early 1870s my great-grandfather, a rabbi, left Lithuania to live in Jerusalem. He did so as an act of pilgrimage to the place that for 3,000 years has been at the heart of Jewish prayer.

But in 1881 something happened to change his life. Pogroms broke out throughout Russia. Suddenly he realized that Europe was no longer safe for Jews. He began to tour the centres of Jewish life, urging people to leave. And in a gesture I still find remarkable, he turned from being a rabbi to becoming a farmer and pioneer. He went to what was then a malaria-ridden swamp, and helped build what became the first new agricultural settlement in the Holy Land. Today, it's a prosperous city. But in its name you can still sense the religious vision of those early settlers. Borrowing a phrase from the prophet Hosea, they called it Petach Tikvah – 'a gateway of hope'.

What was their hope? Not that anyone should be dispossessed, but that together, Jews and Arabs might make that ancient land flower again. Sadly, it didn't happen that way. Twelve years later the Jewish farmers were attacked, and my great-grandfather knew that it was no longer safe to live there and came to Britain. It was an opportunity lost; as so many opportunities have been lost between then and now.

From war, no one gains. From peace, everyone benefits. You see it wherever you look in the pages of history and wherever you travel throughout the world. Why, then, is it so hard to make peace? My great-grandfather would have had a simple answer. Whenever Jews pray, we end with a prayer for peace and at that point we take three steps backward. To make peace you have to make space for someone else. You have to give up a little of your dream for the sake of someone else's dream. I pray that, along with Israel's leaders, Syria's new president has that courage, and that, through the walls of mutual suspicion they finally build the gateway of hope.

INDISCRETIONS

15 May 2000

There I was yesterday morning, reading about the latest series of indiscretions about people in high places. This time they came from a lawyer, no longer alive, once famous for advising the great and the good about how to stay out of the press. Well, he was unwise enough to tell a friend what he thought about some of the people involved, and that friend has now sold the story to the press.

Is *anything* private any more? Probably not, to judge by the sheer number of kiss-and-tell confessions and friend-reveals-all scandals we've had in recent years. Woody Allen once joked, 'They threw me out for cheating in my metaphysics exam. They caught me looking into someone else's soul.' Today, looking into someone else's private life has become our favourite entertainment. Whatever happened to that quaint old saying that 'discretion is the better part of valour'?

I remember once sitting at a dinner next to a distinguished academic I'd asked to be a judge of an award scheme. The ceremony was due to take place the next week. Whatever happens, I said, don't tell anyone who's won. Nobody's supposed to know in advance. To my amazement he proceeded, in a rather loud voice, to name the winner. I said, 'But it's supposed to be a secret.' He said, 'I practice the Oxford way of keeping a secret.' 'What's that?' I asked. He replied, 'You only tell one person at a time.'

Luckily on that occasion no harm was done. But it isn't always the case. Gossip rakes over the reputation of the dead. It plays havoc with relationships between the living. Discretion is to speech what clothes are to the body. Too much nakedness eventually makes us hateful to one another.

Of course, there are truths we need to know; information it's wrong to hide; secrets that ought to be exposed. But not everything's like that. Not for nothing did the Bible teach, 'Don't go round as a gossip among your people' (Lev. 19:16). Those long-lost virtues of reticence and honouring confidences were born out of a desire to protect people and reputations. They cast a veil over the less lovely aspects of the human personality. A world in which people generally think well of one another is better than one in which we suspect that every saint is really a sinner. A cynical society is one that's lost the capacity to admire.

Not everything we hear should we tell, and not everything we know should we sell. Otherwise we'll find we've made a world without friendship, loyalty and trust; and that can't be good news in the long run.

SOCIETY WITH A HUMAN FACE

19 June 2000

This week I'm going to be taking part in a rather unusual conference. It's about religion and welfare, and it'll bring together politicians from all parties, alongside religious leaders, to see how faith-based organizations can help create a caring society.

So, with that in mind, I took a slightly more self-conscious look than usual at what was going on in the synagogue this Saturday. Throughout the week groups of all kinds meet at the synagogue, some for the elderly and those who live alone, others for children and teenagers. It's a place that buzzes with social, educational and welfare activities.

But even on the Sabbath, our day of rest, it was fascinating to see the magic of community at work. In between our prayers and scriptural readings, we took time, as we always do, to register significant moments in the lives of our members. Someone had received an award in the honours list published that morning, so we congratulated him. A young couple had just had a baby, so we sang them a song of congratulation. We said words of consolation to a woman who had just lost her mother; and of course we said prayers for the people who were ill.

Normally I would take these things for granted; but this week I realized what was going on. Each of these individuals was bringing their moment to the community, knowing that a celebration shared is a celebration doubled, and a grief shared is a grief halved.

We make a mistake when we think religion is only about believing. It's also about belonging; and belonging is about community, that delicate yet powerful network of relationships where we learn moral literacy – by being there for other people when they need us, knowing that they'll be there for us when we need them.

In America a research team asked people who they would turn to if a member of their family needed help. Twenty-five per cent said: a government agency. Eighty-six per cent said: a member of their congregation. Perhaps that's a measure of how strongly places of worship sustain community; and how important that is to our sense of not being alone.

I love our congregations because they're almost the only place nowadays where rich and poor, old and young, meet in equal dignity and mutual responsibility. For me, community is the place where they know your name and where they miss you when you're not there. It's society with a human face, and that's a source of welfare no government can reproduce.

THE JOURNEY TO FREEDOM

21 April 1997

It's been a very odd election campaign so far. We've had the chickens, headless or otherwise, a British lion and now a British bulldog, and some dark mutterings about a European creature called EMU, all of which have given a new meaning to Aristotle's phrase, 'political animal'. But beneath the fun and fight and spin, there's been some disturbing evidence that people are getting bored with, or even cynical about, politics; and that many young people just won't vote. Perhaps that's because a free society is a bit like health. When it's there we take it for granted. It's only when we're in danger of losing it that we become really conscious of how important it is.

Which is why, starting this evening, the Jewish community will be celebrating our most ancient festival, Pesach, the Passover. These are the days when we remember the story of the biblical book of Exodus, of how the Israelites were once slaves, and were rescued by God and set out across the wilderness towards freedom. We don't just tell the story. We live it. We eat the *matzah*, the unleavened bread of affliction. We taste the *maror*, the bitter herbs of persecution. And we drink four cups of wine by way of making a blessing over liberty. And the whole service, which takes place at home, revolves around the questions asked by the youngest child there. *Mah nishtanah halaylah hazeh*, why is this night different? The events we'll be speaking about took place more than 3,000 years ago; but we recall them as if they happened yesterday, because freedom needs to be cherished in every generation. And what Passover suggests is that the best way of doing so is to remember once in a while what it feels like not to be free.

So when it comes to a general election, religious faith may not tell us which way to vote, but it can tell us why voting matters. Democratic politics is driven by one of the noblest of all ideals, and its seed was planted in the Bible, even if it took many centuries to grow. Passover taught us that God values human freedom, and wants us to create societies in which it is respected. That means government by consent, answerable to us, the governed. It was Charles Peguy who said, 'All things begin in mysticism and end in politics.' That's certainly true of the vision of a free society, born all those years ago in the exodus on Pesach. So as 1 May draws near, I for one give thanks for the right to vote, and for this our latest stage in the long road to freedom.

THE TALE OF OUR YESTERDAYS

3 April 1996

This evening my wife and I will be sitting down with our children and telling each other one of the oldest stories in the world: the story of Passover, Pesach, the Jewish festival of freedom. It isn't exactly *Thought for the Day* material. No mad cows, no battling politicians. Topical, it isn't.

It's about how a group of slaves, the ancient Israelites, left Egypt to begin the long march across the desert towards the promised land. And to make it more than just a story we add a touch of drama, a bit of virtual reality. We eat *matzah*, the unleavened bread, as if we were there in the desert. We eat *maror*, bitter herbs, as if the taste of slavery were still fresh in our mouths. And we drink four cups of wine, each signifying a stage on the road to freedom. In fact, we celebrate Pesach more or less as the Israelites must have done more than 3,000 years ago, and as Jews have done ever since.

I suppose the question is why. Do we really need to recall a past so ancient, and take so much trouble to teach it to our children?

Speaking personally, I owe my parents a huge debt of thanks for teaching me the story, the songs, the rituals and the questions: *Mah nishtanah halaylah hazeh*, why is this night different from all other nights?

It took me a long time to realize what was happening on those Passover evenings. I was being helped to learn who I was and the history of the people of whom I was a part. I was discovering the values that sustained my ancestors in tough times: trust, a passion for freedom and justice, a willingness to ask and learn. I was joining the great conversation between the generations, which is what education ought to be. And the best thing was, it was fun.

There's a lot to be said for switching off the television once in a while and talking to our children about the journey we and those who came before us have taken, and what we learned on the way.

In fact, sometimes we have too little confidence as parents. We underestimate how much our children want to hear from us the stories that give sense and purpose to our lives, and will one day give them strength. Jews never lost the habit of telling the story to their children. Perhaps that's why we survived.

Values aren't invented. They're the work of many generations. And that's why we have to hand them on to our children. Sometimes the tale of all our yesterdays is the best thought for today.

A CANDLE OF HOPE

10 December 2001

Today is the first day of Hanukkah, the Jewish festival of lights. And I want to tell the story of the festival, because of what it tells us about our post-September 11 world.

Hanukkah happened some two centuries before the birth of Christianity. Israel was then under the rule of the empire of Alexander the Great. A ruler came to power – Antiochus IV – who was determined to impose his values on the Jewish people. He forbade the public practice of Judaism, set up a statue of Zeus in the Temple, and systematically desecrated Jerusalem's holy sites. This was tyranny on a grand scale, and had he succeeded, not only would Judaism have died, but also there would have been no Christianity or Islam.

A small group of Jews rose in revolt, and, astonishingly, in the space of three years, defeated the Greek army, restored religious liberty and reconsecrated the Temple. Hanukkah means 'reconsecration'.

Yet, oddly enough, when we recall Hanukkah we tell a different, and apparently more minor story of how, searching through the wreckage of the Temple, Jews found a single cruse of oil still undefiled. With it they were able to relight the *menorah*, the Temple candelabrum; and the oil just kept on burning, which is why we still we light candles in our homes at this time of the year. The military victory was extraordinary; yet it didn't last. Two hundred and thirty years later, the Temple was destroyed, this time by the Romans. What lasted was the spiritual miracle, the faith which, like the oil, was inextinguishable.

This year's military campaign in Afghanistan has been a success. A tyrannical regime has been overthrown. It isn't over yet, but already many freedoms have been restored, even if at a heavy cost in human life. But what Hanukkah tells us is that it isn't always the big events that make a difference in the long run. It's sometimes the small miracle that endures.

It won't be a military victory that will change our world. Instead it will be whether we in the affluent West are willing to share some of our blessings with the three-quarters of humanity who today live in poverty, hunger and disease. They have so little; we have so much; and it doesn't take much to rescue a life from despair. Military victories are temporary; it's the spiritual achievements that last. The real test of our age will be whether, for those who suffer in the dark places of the world, we can light a candle of hope.

REMBRANDT AND THE TURNER PRIZE

10 December 2003

My attention was caught this week by two contrasting stories from the world of art. The first was the Tate Gallery's Turner Prize, awarded to a potter whose work was described in the press as specializing in pornographic and paedophile imagery with titles like 'We've found the body of your child' – worthy company for such previous winners as the unmade bed, the elephant dung and, of course, the pickled sheep.

What, I wonder, will future ages make of these works? Will they see them as we today see the impressionists, scandalous in their time but now a paradigm of beauty? Or will they perhaps see them as symbols of an age confused as to the role and significance of art?

Which brings me to the second story, the publication this week of a book called *Rembrandt's Jews*. It tells of how the great seventeenth-century Dutch painter was fascinated by the Jews he met in Amsterdam, most of them refugees from religious persecution in Spain. There is something wondrous in the way those portraits bring out the beauty of those whom others so often despised.

One of the great mystics of the twentieth century, Rabbi Abraham Kook, was stranded in London during the First World War, and he found inspiration by going, as often as he could, to the National Gallery to look at its Rembrandts, and he said about them something very striking.

The Bible says that on the first day God created light. But He didn't make the sun and moon until the fourth day. What then was the light of day one? The sages said it was a special radiance that God kept for the righteous in ages to come. God took some of that light, said Rabbi Kook, and gave it to Rembrandt.

I think I understand what he meant. There is something religious about great art. The late Iris Murdoch used to speak about its power to do what she called 'unselfing' – to release us from the prison of our cares and look for a moment with awe and gratitude and, yes, humility, at the sheer miracle of that which is there, frozen in a moment of eternity.

Which is, I think, the difference between art then and now. Art which aims to shock, shocks only once, while art which aims at beauty never fades. Art as sensation eventually deadens our sensations, while art as wonder wakens them. Which is why I'll leave the Turner to higher minds, and be grateful simply for Rembrandt and his undiminished gift to re-enchant our disenchanted world.

TWO BOOKS OF LIFE

11 June 2001

A few days ago I paid a visit to Lord Robert Winston, one of Britain's best-known medical scientists, to see some of the work being done in the new research unit at the Hammersmith Hospital. It's an extraordinary experience seeing the latest techniques in *in vitro* fertilization, and cutting-edge research into embryo development and the human genome. I can't say I understood it all, but I did get a sense of the sheer excitement of decoding the book of life, and coming ever closer to being able to treat at least some genetic disease and disability. It's all very futuristic stuff.

And now I'm here in Glasgow to celebrate, among other things, the completion of two Torah scrolls, the Five Books of Moses, still written as were the Dead Sea Scrolls more than 2,000 years ago; by hand, with a quill, on parchment – a living link with the ancient past. And we danced with the scrolls just as King David did 3,000 years ago when he brought the ark to Jerusalem.

And what struck me was not only the contrast between these two events, but also the connection, because there in Lord Winston's office, wedged in between the latest scientific research, I saw a copy of the Five Books of Moses, together with several volumes of commentary. Lord Winston is an Orthodox Jew and his faith guides his work.

Ours is a very future-oriented religion. We're not afraid of new technologies, precisely because they allow us to fulfil, in ways undreamt of by our ancestors, some very ancient mandates indeed: to cure disease, treat infertility, and to become, in that lovely Jewish phrase, 'God's partners in the work of creation'.

And that's what struck me in these two encounters, one with

tomorrow's world of medicine, the other with the faith of yester-day. Religion doesn't mean living *in* the past, it means living *with* the past – taking the message of those ancient scrolls with us as we journey into that undiscovered country called the future.

The biggest mistake we could possibly make in the twenty-first century is to believe that embracing the future means jettisoning the past. Our scientific knowledge changes daily. It's constantly growing, always new. But our human situation doesn't change. We still need the guidance of our ancestors and the voice of God, and the more power we have to heal or harm, mend or destroy, the more we need those ancient truths reminding us of human dignity and the sanctity of life, our responsibility as guardians of creation. Those most at home in the wisdom of the past can best face the future without fear.

WHAT WE TEACH OUR CHILDREN

11 April 2003

Rarely have I felt more strongly than I have these past two days the connection between the now of the news and the then of religious memory. On the one hand those remarkable images from Baghdad: Allied tanks in front of presidential palaces, scenes of jubilation on the streets, that defining image of Saddam's statue toppling and falling – massive and seemingly strong on the outside but empty of all human content within. That's freedom now.

But at the same time, in Jewish homes throughout the country, we've been getting ready for Passover, the festival in which we re-enact another moment of liberation 3,300 years ago when in the days of Moses the Israelites prepared to say goodbye to their own experience of tyranny. That's freedom then.

And the connection between them is deep and real. For me it's summed up in the moment when Moses addresses the Israelites on the brink of the exodus: in the twelfth and thirteenth chapters of the book of Exodus. Moses does a surprising thing. He doesn't talk about liberation or about a golden future, the 'land flowing with milk and honey'. He doesn't even talk about the difficulties that lie ahead, what Nelson Mandela called the 'Long Walk to Freedom'. Instead, three times, he talks about parents and children and the duty to hand the story on to future generations, which is what we do on Passover to this day. It's one of the deepest of all insights into what it takes to make a free society.

Freedom – Moses was saying – doesn't come in a day. It's the work of a lifetime, many lifetimes. And what counts is the story we tell our children. To defeat a tyrant you need an army; but to defeat tyranny you need education. Every year you and your children must taste the unleavened bread of affliction and the bitter herbs of persecution so that future generations never take liberty for granted. Freedom may be won on the battlefield but it's sustained in the human heart. Therefore, said Moses, don't just celebrate; educate.

I give thanks for the courage of those who fought this war; and offer prayers for the people of Iraq that they may celebrate their own festival of freedom. But there's still too much hatred out there in the world, too much rage and readiness to resort to violence. So I have one more prayer this Passover: that the nations of the world finally acknowledge that what we teach children tomorrow is as important as the victories we celebrate today.

WHEN WORDS FAIL

11 June 2003

Those involved in the current drive for peace between Israel and the Palestinians call it the Road Map. But there's a difference between a road and a map. On a map everything is clear. It's when you take to the road that things get complicated. There are traffic jams, diversions and delays. That's when you need more than a map. You need patience, the ability to live through a hundred setbacks and still keep going. That's what both sides need right now.

So far the signs are good. After the Gulf War in 1991, a historic ten year peace process began: first Madrid, then Oslo, then Camp David and Taba. Never before had the two sides been so close. Tragically, that process collapsed into violence – and now, two and three-quarter years later we can see what it brought. Nothing – except for the hundreds dead and thousands injured on both sides, leaving wounds that will take years to heal. And now, after the Second Gulf War, the two sides have come together again. Leaders on both sides have taken significant steps, saying things their followers never thought they'd say, and taking great risks in doing so. So far the signs are good.

But there's one obstacle still to be overcome. The single greatest mistake, and it's been made many times in history, is to believe that peace is a zero-sum game. If I win, you lose. If I suffer, you gain. It isn't so. The truth is the opposite. From violence both sides suffer. From peace, both sides gain. That is why no one does a service to peace by demonizing one side and making heroes of the other. Peace is a duet scored for two voices; and someone who thinks that one voice can win by drowning out the other just hasn't understood what a duet is.

There's an extraordinary verse early in the Bible that's invariably mistranslated. Read literally it says this: 'And Cain said to his brother Abel; and it came to pass that when they were in the field Cain rose against his brother Abel and killed him.'

The syntax is fractured. Cain said – but the Bible doesn't say what he said. The sentence breaks off midway, and the message is as sharp as a jagged edge. When conversation fails, violence begins; and violence has no victors, only victims. That's why as well as a road map, both sides need to commit themselves, whatever else happens, to keep on talking. Wars are won by weapons. Peace is won by words.

WHERE TERROR IS DEFEATED

11 September 2003

Today is the second anniversary of 9/11, the day that changed the world, and which of us will ever forget it? Looking back on that day two years ago, I think of the courage, the heroism, the simple humanity it called forth. I think of the New York firemen, so many of whom lost their lives saving lives. I think of the passengers on the fourth plane, Flight 93, who fought back and crashed their plane into a field so that others would not die, and of the thousands who tended the wounded, comforted the bereaved, and gave shelter to those who were stranded. It was they who in the midst of terror gave birth to hope, because compassion runs deeper than hate, and the human instinct for freedom will always eventually win against those whose idea of conflict resolution is to kill those with whom they disagree.

But terror has not yet been defeated. Since then there have been deadly attacks in India, Pakistan, Tunisia, the Philippines, Bali, Mombassa, Yemen, Kuwait, Casablanca, and the list goes on. Thirty-six hours ago a friend of my brother was sitting in a cafe in Jerusalem. His name was David Applebaum, a hero who dedicated his life to saving the lives of others. He headed Jerusalem's emergency medical service treating all victims of terror, regardless of race or creed. Yesterday should have been the happiest day of his life. His daughter was getting married, and the night before the ceremony he had taken her out for a coffee when the bomb went off. Yesterday instead of the wedding, both of them were buried.

If anything is evil, terror is. It strikes the young, the old, the innocent. It is destruction for destruction's sake. It never achieved anything that could not have been achieved by diplomacy or peaceful protest. And terrorists always end up harming their own people and their cause. One who dies for the sake of faith is called a martyr. But one who kills for the sake of faith is a blasphemer, because he or she desecrates the one thing on which God has set his image, life itself. And so, two years later the world still needs our prayers: for comfort for the bereaved and healing for the wounded. Above all, it needs all of us to say in the name of our respective faiths that deliberate killing of the innocent is evil, whoever does it, whoever it is done against. Terror must be defeated in the human heart if it is to be defeated in our suddenly vulnerable world.

TO CHOOSE TO HAVE A CHILD

12 April 1995

In one of yesterday's papers I saw a headline that should surely give us pause for thought. It read: 'Babies, who needs them?' It continued: 'They've said no to domesticity, and no to traditional relationships. Now one in five women is saying no to mother-hood.'

The story was about a report published this week showing that the number of childless women has doubled in the space of a single generation. Of course, some are simply unable to have children, and our hearts go out to them. But that can't be the whole story because our techniques of treating infertility have got significantly better over the last twenty years. It seems, from the report, that more and more women are quite simply choosing not to have chil-dren.

That in itself shouldn't surprise us. Medical techniques have made parenthood much more a matter of choice than it used to be. And understandably, more women are choosing to have relat-ionships and careers without wanting to be tied to babies and to home. But just because it's become a matter of choice, we need to think again about why we make the choice to have children.

In three days time, Jews throughout the world will be celebrating the festival of Passover, the time in which we tell the story of our beginnings as a people, about how we were once slaves in Egypt and began the long journey across the wilderness to freedom.

And more than most, it's a festival about children. The great ritual of Passover, the *seder* service, takes place at home, and it begins with the youngest child asking the four questions about why this night is different from all other nights. It's a time when we celebrate the family, and the passing on of memory from one generation to the next. In the Bible itself Moses repeatedly says that the most important thing about the exodus is the way we teach it to our children. And to this day, on Passover, Jewish children know that they are the centre of attention.

Why? I suppose it's because if we care for something beyond ourselves, we want it to continue. It matters that something of us will live on after us. Having a child is, in a sense, the most extraordinary thing a human being can do. To bring new life into the world, to protect and care for it, and to know that in this new life we come as near as most of us will know to immortality: these are not small things. And perhaps the secret of Jewish survival through 4,000 years lies in the fact that we've always tried to put children first.

The fact that we can now choose not to, may one day lead us to think again and realize what a precious thing it is that we can choose to have children.

THE WARSAW GHETTO

13 April 1995

Tomorrow night, throughout the world, Jews will be celebrating one of the most powerful religious ceremonies of the year, the *seder* service of Passover. It's a time when we gather in our extended families and tell the story of the exodus from Egypt more than 3,000 years ago.

We do more than tell it. We relive it. We eat the unleavened bread of affliction. We taste the bitter herbs of slavery. And we drink four cups of the wine of freedom. I know of few other occasions in which history is made to come so vividly alive. You feel as if you were there. As part of the service we say: in every generation each of us must feel as if we personally left Egypt. And we do. On Passover we turn history into living memory. But why is it so important to remember what happened so long ago?

When people ask me that, I think back to something that occurred on the eve of Passover fifty-two years ago. The Jews of Europe were being murdered in their millions. In Warsaw, in the ghetto, only a fifth of the Jews were still alive. The rest had been deported to the concentration camps. Then the news came through. The remaining Jews were to be killed the next day. Instead of the festival of freedom, they were to receive the decree of death.

What happened next was one of the most remarkable stories of the Second World War. The Jews fought back. It was a hopeless struggle: 1,200 Jewish fighters, with a few smuggled arms, surrounded by German troops and tanks. They knew they would lose and that few would survive. But fight they did, for days and weeks, until June. As an act of resistance it was extraordinary.

On the first night, the survivors of the ghetto sat down amidst the wreckage and celebrated Passover. Rarely can the ancient story of slavery and liberation have resonated with such power, giving those who heard it the strength to live and die for the cause of freedom. They knew it was their story.

In a few weeks time, we'll commemorate the fiftieth anniversary of VE Day. And those like me who were born after that event sometimes ask: why remember?

But Passover gives us the answer. If we are to cherish freedom, and to guard it, we must remember what the alternative is: the bread of affliction and the bitter herbs of slavery. Each new generation learn now how freedom was fought for, and painfully won. Memory is our best guardian of liberty.

PARENTHOOD AS PRIVILEGE

13 December 2002

Yesterday, education secretary Charles Clarke announced that in future, headteachers who request it will be given powers to fine parents whose children consistently play truant from school. Discipline, he said, begins at home. The announcement will spark controversy; but it did something important, namely, to raise the question: what are the responsibilities of parents?

Today in the West we're engaged in an experiment that's never been tried before, a world where marriage is optional, stable families increasingly rare, and where almost all the responsibilities of parenthood can be delegated away: education to schools, law enforcement to the police, and care to child minders or welfare agencies. In America the average child spends four hours a day watching television, and only forty minutes a week talking to its parents. In the words of Robert Reich, the family, like the business corporation, is being downsized and outsourced. Rarely has parenthood been surrounded by so much confusion or held in such low esteem. And that's bad news.

One of the most beautiful things the Hebrew Bible gave the world was the idea that God isn't just a power but also a parent. We call him our father. Or, as God said through the prophet Isaiah, 'Like one whom his mother comforts, so will I comfort you.' I love the comment of one new mother who said: 'Since I've become a parent I can relate much more closely to God. Now I know what it's like to create something you can't control.' And in the one verse in the entire Bible which explains why God chose Abraham to be the founder of a new faith, it says, 'I have chosen him so that he will teach his children and his household after him to keep the way of the Lord, doing what is right and just.' What made Abraham and Sarah special in God's eyes was simply that they understood the responsibilities of parenthood.

Without the help of parents, even the best school and the finest teachers may fail. Even the most gifted child may face emotional difficulties. I know that what I most loved about my parents was that gave they us, their children, time. When we did well we knew we were giving them pride. There is no more awesome responsibility than bringing new life into the world, and having done so we can't just walk away and leave the rest to others. It isn't just discipline, but much else besides, that begins at home. Which is why we have to rediscover the truth that parenthood isn't a burden but the greatest privilege of all.

PEACE AS A PARADOX

13 September 2002

In January this year I stood at Ground Zero, awed by the sheer scale of the destruction, moved by the messages from those who lost family or friends. I was there together with leaders of all the world's great faiths. The Archbishop of Canterbury said a prayer. So did a Muslim imam. The Chief Rabbi of Israel read a reflection. A Hindu sprinkled holy water from the Ganges. And I was struck by the sheer dissonance between this coming together of faiths in peace and the terrible religious extremism of those who planned and carried out the attack. Religion, I suddenly realized, is like fire. It warms, but it also burns, and we are the guardians of the flame.

Religion, far from dying, remains a significant factor in conflict zones throughout the world – Northern Ireland, the Balkans, the Middle East, Kashmir – because, whereas the twentieth century was about the politics of ideology, the twenty-first century is about the politics of identity. Who am I and to which side do I belong? And to those questions, the great religions are our oldest and deepest answer. The trouble is that the politics of identity is inherently divisive because by creating an 'us' it also creates a 'them', the people not like us: the unredeemed, the infidel, those outside our circle of belonging. Which is why peace is so hard across the great divide of different faiths.

Peace is a paradox. Almost all the great religions praise it, and decry conflict and war. Yet those who show courage in battle are celebrated, while those who take risks for peace are often assassinated – Lincoln, Gandhi, Martin Luther King, Anwar Sadat and Yitzhak Rabin. War speaks to our sense of identity. There's an 'us' and a 'them' and no possibility of confusing the two. But peace involves a profound crisis of identity. When enemies shake hands, who is now the 'us' and who the 'them'? That is why the pursuit of peace can sometimes seem like a kind of betrayal.

Which is why, as this century unfolds, we're going to need not just military strength but also spiritual courage, to reach out a hand of friendship across boundaries, to recognize the integrity of ways of life unlike our own, to listen to other people's stories and to see the trace of God in the face of a stranger. God has made many faiths, but only one world in which to live together. And it's getting smaller all the time.

TEMPORARY RESIDENTS

15 February 2002

A report published yesterday urges the government to adopt a more environmentally friendly energy policy, by way of more heat efficient homes, and a greater use of renewable energy sources like the sun, the wind and the waves. I must say that at this time of the morning and the week I could do with some renewable energy, but the point is serious and urgent.

We're using up our coal, oil and gas at a prodigious rate; and in the process we're not just polluting the environment and damaging the earth's atmosphere. We're also buying the present at the cost of the future. Unlike wind, solar and tidal energy, the fossil fuels we burn now won't be there for our grandchildren not yet born.

And it's here, I think, that a biblical perspective is helpful. In Genesis 1 we read of how humanity was told to fill the earth and subdue it, our mandate for science and technology. But in Genesis 2 we're told that man was placed in the garden to serve and protect it, meaning that nature has its own integrity that we must respect and preserve.

The line that always resonates with me is that remarkable verse in which God says, 'The land shall not be sold in perpetuity for the earth is Mine; you are only temporary residents.' What this means is that we don't own nature; at most we hold it in trust on behalf of God who made it, and the future generations who will inhabit it. Hence all those laws in the Bible – don't work the land on the seventh day and the seventh year; don't mix different species; don't destroy fruit trees in the course of war – possibly the world's first environmental legislation.

It took the modern prophets of ecology, the green activists, to make us go back to the Bible and realize what it was whispering to us all those centuries ago. We're the guests of nature, the guardians of creation; not the owners who can do with it what we like.

There's a lovely rabbinic comment, dating back at least fifteen hundred years, that might have been made for yesterday's report. When, at the end of creation, God made man, he showed him all the glories of nature. See the beauty of the world, he said, and I have handed it over to you. But be careful that you do not damage it, for if you do, there will be no one left to mend what you destroyed. Don't use up what you can't renew.

THE CAPTURE OF SADDAM HUSSEIN

17 December 2003

In two days time we'll begin celebrating Hanukkah, the Jewish festival of lights, best known for our custom of lighting for eight days the candelabrum we call the *menorah*, symbol of the one that once stood in the temple in Jerusalem. The interesting thing about Hanukkah, though, is the way its significance changed over time.

We can read the first draft of the story in the first and second books of Maccabees. They tell of how Antiochus IV, one of the rulers of the Alexandrian empire, forbade the public practice of Judaism and erected pagan statues in the temple. The Jews rose in revolt and won the most remarkable military victory in the history of ancient Judaism. They reconquered Jerusalem, reconsecrated the Temple, and recovered their freedom.

Yet the books of Maccabees never made it into the Bible, because the military victory was short lived. Within a century Israel was again under foreign rule, this time the Romans, and 130 years after that the Temple was destroyed. Had that been the whole story, there would today be no Hanukkah, perhaps no Judaism.

What lasted wasn't the military victory but the religious one. Within a century Jews had transformed themselves from a people organized around kings, soldiers and power into a faith built on home, school and synagogue. The Hanukkah lights came to represent the words of the prophet Zechariah: not by might nor by force but by my spirit, says God.

Hanukkah holds a message of hope for the people of Iraq. The capture of Saddam Hussein means that the military campaign has effectively reached closure. It doesn't mean that violence will end. Tragically, there will be more terror, suicide bombings and tensions between the different religious groups and ethnic populations that make up Iraq.

But the question now will be: can Iraq begin the long journey to a free, civil, and ultimately democratic society? And that can't be answered by outside forces, the United States or the United Nations. It can only be answered by the Iraqis themselves.

What Hanukkah tells us is that military victories are short lived. What matters in the long run are habits of the heart. Can we respect the freedoms of others as well as our own? Can we pursue peace, not just power? That depends on what we teach the next generation in our homes, schools and houses of worship.

So this Hanukkah I'll say a prayer for the brave and battered people of Iraq. May they too see the last flames of war light a lasting candle of peace.

WHY TERROR ALWAYS FAILS

17 September 2001

On the eve of the Jewish New Year, I, like so many of us, am still in a state of shock. As long as I live, I'll never forget those television pictures of a nightmare become real, including last night's aerial views of the full extent of the devastation. We've seen the very worst in humanity: a brutal act of naked evil. But we've also seen the very best, in countless acts of support and human kindness. And today we'll see the sheer power of human resilience, as people follow President Bush's call to return to work and reconnect with normal life again.

And that is why acts of terror, though they succeed for a moment, always fail in the end. Those who commit them believe they can create panic and fear. But after the initial shock, free human beings don't react with panic and fear. Their response is to try to help, to rescue, to comfort, to heal.

Will we ever forget those passengers on the fourth plane, who fought with the hijackers at the certain cost of their own lives, to save the lives of people on the ground? Will we ever forget those last telephoned messages of love from those who knew they were about to die? Or the tidal wave of shared emotion as people heard the news and were instantly united with the injured and bereaved in grief and prayer? Or the tears shed at the first funerals, over the weekend, as firemen mourned their colleagues who gave their lives to rescue others?

If ever we sought proof of the power of the human spirit, it's been there, in the bond of solidarity and compassion that, from New York to New Zealand, turned strangers into friends and bystanders into a single extended family. It's as if the world had put its arms around America and given it comfort in the hour of its grief. And in that moment, a new hope was born: that together we can defeat the forces of death and find a way, however painful and difficult, to a new affirmation and defence of life.

And when, last Wednesday, I stood together with Muslim and Christian leaders, expressing our grief and our joint commitment to peace, I knew just this: that love is stronger than hate; freedom more powerful than its enemies; and the human spirit too resilient to be intimidated for long. And so I pray, in words adapted from the liturgy of the New Year: 'O God of life, whose gift is life, be with us now and in the coming year, giving us the courage to affirm and cherish life.'

THE BLAME GAME

18 December 2000

Oh dear, here we are again, taking part in the nation's favourite indoor sport, 'Who's to blame?' This time the subject is law and order, in the wake of the tragic Demilola killing, the continuing echoes of the Macpherson Report, and various accusations and counter-accusations that have been flying around for the past few days.

Some blame the media, others blame society. For some it's all the fault of a liberal elite, for others it's the fault of an authoritarian counter-elite. And of course everyone blames the police – for being too tough or not tough enough, too politically correct or incorrect.

It all reminds me of the Bible teacher who spent a year trying to teach a rather rowdy class the book of Joshua, and at the end of it he asked the simplest question he could think of: 'Tell me, who destroyed the walls of Jericho.' And from the back of the room little Marvin put his hand up and said, 'Please sir, it wasn't me.' That's the essence of the blame game: whatever's going wrong, it's someone else's fault. Please sir, it wasn't me.

In fact, the Bible has a profound commentary on this – because the blame game is the oldest human story of all. It begins with the first man and woman together in paradise. The first thing God tells them is not to eat a certain fruit; and of course the first thing they do is to eat it. And when God asks, 'What's going on?', the man blames the woman; the woman blames the serpent; and the result is that they all get thrown out of Eden. 'Please sir, it wasn't me' is the quickest route to Paradise Lost.

What's fascinating is that in the very next verse, Adam turns to his wife and gives her a new name, Eve, 'because she is the mother of all life'. And my interpretation of that verse is this. At first Adam was distraught, because he thought he'd just lost immortality. He would no longer live for ever. But then he realized: no, that's not so. I can live on, not in myself but through my children. But having children is not something I can do alone. That is only something I can do in partnership with my wife. He stopped blaming her and instead began to see that they could create something lasting, but only together.

And that's the only way we can fight and defeat crime – together, as families and communities, not blaming the police but helping them; because neither they nor we can do it alone.

THINKING GLOBAL

18 June 2001

Yet again, this time at Gothenburg, an international gathering has become a scene of protest and violence – three shot, seventy injured, 500 arrested. It's easy to dismiss these demonstrations as the work of anarchists, but that's not all they are. The issues they raise concern us all – the environment, nuclear weapons, international corporations and world trade. And what they have in common is that they expose two weaknesses at the very heart of our political situation.

First, they're global, which means they need cooperation far beyond the boundaries of individual countries. For two centuries the dominant political force was the nation-state. But today the nation-state has become too big for the small problems and too small for the big ones. The trouble is that when you create international decision-making bodies, you move politics beyond the point at which our votes make a difference, which is why fewer people vote at elections.

The other problem is that so many of the issues that affect us are long term. They're about the choice between which path to take, where the results of those choices may not be clear for a decade or even a century. Yet the attention span of politics rarely extends beyond the next election. How do you get a short-term enterprise to think and act in long-term ways?

The result is a world which feels like a car travelling at great speed with no one quite sure where it's going and too many hands on the wheel, none of them ours.

Now the last thing I'd suggest is to turn these decisions over to religious leaders; but the great faiths do have something to teach us about our present situation. First, they're long term. There's nothing longer than the long biblical journey to redemption. Second, they're international. Globalization may be a new word in secular terms, but for at least 2,000 years Jews have been scattered across the globe, yet they saw themselves as one people with a strong sense of collective responsibility. Third, they're close to people; they're about local communities where individuals matter. And fourth, they ask the big questions: what kind of world do we seek to create? And what kind of world is it where the few live in affluence and the many die in poverty?

A true global politics will begin, not with the clash of national interests, but with a greater over-arching truth; that we are one family under the parenthood of God, guardians of His world for the sake of generations not yet born.

LEFT ALONE OR KEPT INFORMED?

18 June 2003

There's been quite a controversy over yesterday's suggestion, by a House of Commons Committee, that there should be a law protecting individuals from over-intrusive media. Is there, or should there be, a right to privacy?

It's an area that can give rise to strange situations. An American friend of mine was involved in such a case some years ago. He was a professor of theology who'd given an extremely highbrow lecture, part of which was shown, without his consent, in a Hollywood gangster film, in a way that made him look a bit ridiculous. Well, he took the film company to court, and apparently in American law, if you're a public figure, you're held to be fair game. The result was that the lawyers on the opposing side claimed that he was virtually a household name, whereas his own lawyers had to prove that no one had ever heard of him. There are times when you don't know whether it's better to win or lose.

And that's what makes many privacy cases so paradoxical. How should we feel about someone who spends most of his or her life *seeking* publicity, and then complaining when they get it, but not on their own terms? And how should we balance concern for privacy against our no less genuine need for a free press, on which a free society depends?

The Hebrew Bible is quite clear. Yes, there is such a thing in Judaism as a duty to respect privacy – the rabbis said that one should rather throw oneself into a fiery furnace than shame someone else in public. But the Bible does not spare us from some quite intimate glimpses into the private lives of its heroes. The story of King David and Bathesheba, for example, is told with relentless honesty, and David offers no defence on the grounds that his private life was, if you'll excuse the pun, his own affair.

What makes the Bible so powerful is that it holds no one above criticism; and the role of the press now, like that of the prophets then, is to expose the corruptions of power. The real difference is between public interest and prurience, what we need to know, and what we have a merely voyeuristic wish to see. A politician's failings are one thing; a sunbathing superstar another. It should not be impossible to frame a code of conduct that is fair, protective of rich and poor alike, and draws the delicate but necessary line between our private right to be left alone and our collective right to be informed.

PROFITS AND PROPHETS

19 March 2001

You're in a shop and the person at the till gives you ten pounds too much in change. Do you thank your lucky stars or give it back? There's a job you want, but you don't have all the qualifications. Do you risk a little creative fiction on your application form, or do you tell the truth and take your chance? You're short of money and you could get some by massaging your expense account. It wouldn't make much difference to the company but it would make a big difference to you. What do you do? Most of us face decisions like these, and it matters to us as individuals, and collectively as a society, whether we do what's right, or simply what we think we can get away with.

Which is why, in two days time, the Secretary of State for Education, David Blunkett, and I, will be launching a new curriculum for schools, called 'Money and Morals'. It's about ethics in the workplace and the market place, and it's been put together by one of the organizations I'm proudest of having a share in: the Jewish Association of Business Ethics.

We launched it just under ten years ago, in the belief that business really is a moral enterprise. I know that might sound odd, if you believe that companies are simply there to make money, that business is a game in which winner takes all, and ethics is for wimps. But that's not what I've learned from the most successful business people I've known. Yes, they say, you can make a quick profit by being unscrupulous; but it never lasts, and you lose in the end. Real success depends on fairness to customers, decency to employees, quality in what you sell and integrity in how you sell it. Or, as one of the country's leading financial journalists told me:

'It's all in the Bible really – fair weights, fair measures, decency to the people you work with, and above all integrity, or what the Bible calls justice.'

So, having taken ethical debate into some of our leading boardrooms, we're now taking it to schools. It's an imaginative project; not preachy or judgemental. It's based on case studies put together by business people and financial journalists to reflect the real world. And a survey of 34,000 teenagers in England and Wales tells us that education does make a difference. Children who've been exposed to strong ethical guidelines do act with more honesty and responsibility. For once biblical prophets and company profits coincide. Morality works; which is why work needs a moral sense.

THE WORLD UPSIDE DOWN

1 January 2004

Goodbye 2003. You tried your best but, rugby aside, you weren't a vintage year. It was the year of war in Iraq and earthquake in Iran; the year when both Vladimir Putin and George Bush paid state visits to Britain, reminding us how much the political landscape has changed, but also of violence in Zimbabwe and terror in Istanbul, reminding us how much has stayed the same. May saw the Road Map to peace in the Middle East, but it also saw the publication of a road map of London printed upside down, with south at the top, presumably for the benefit of people who see the world upside down.

And – do you know – perhaps we do. I have a little experiment I sometimes do when giving a lecture on happiness. I hold up a sheet of blank paper with a black dot in the middle and ask people what they see. They say: a black dot. I then point out that the dot is less than one per cent of the page. What they've missed is the ninety-nine per cent of the paper that's clear and clean.

Which is why the bad news is news while the good news rarely is. We're genetically conditioned to notice things that are odd, discrepant, out of place. The very fact that we notice the bad tells us that we are surrounded by good. It's just that we don't notice it, the way we don't notice the clear paper around the black dot. If good news ever became news, *then* we'd have reason to worry.

So this year, why not try seeing the world the right way up. Go somewhere without your mobile phone. Watch children in a park kicking up the leaves and remember what the world once looked like when you were that age, and know that *it* hasn't changed; why then should you? When you're caught in a traffic jam, smile. It'll cheer you up, infuriate everyone else, and remind you that humour is always more human than rage. Next time you're bombarded by advertisements telling you what you don't yet have, remind yourself of what you do: the sheer miracle that we are here, the world is here, and we have the privilege to see it.

Breathe and let the stillness of the turning world steal over you. Remember that not the least of God's creative acts was to see the world, that it is good. Or as W. H. Auden put it in a lovely line: 'In the prison of his days, teach the free man how to praise.'

SPIKE

1 March 2002

I'm going to miss Spike Milligan, that zany, anarchic, lovable comedian who died two days ago. He was, of course, the creator of the 'The Goon Show', and which of us who were children in the 50s didn't wait for it to come round each week, with its surreal plots and crazy characters, Harry Secombe as Neddy Seagoon, Peter Sellers as Major Bloodnok, Spike himself as Eccles, and Count Moriarty. Most of us in those days, from my schoolmates to the Prince of Wales, used to spend much of our time doing excruciating Goon impressions, and only my respect for the BBC stops me from doing one now. I've no doubt that right now in heaven he's keeping the angels entertained. Meanwhile down here on earth he kept his last joke to the end. He asked that on his tombstone should be engraved the words, 'Here lies Spike Milligan. I told you I was ill.'

I didn't know, until I read his obituary yesterday, that he suffered from manic depression and had at least ten serious mental breakdowns. But I might have guessed. There's a certain kind of humour that only comes from deep pain, and the fact that he lived well into his eighties suggests that maybe it did more than make us laugh. It kept him alive.

It was the American sociologist Peter Berger who called humour a signal of transcendence and actually wrote a book about its religious significance. He called it *Redeeming Laughter*. What I think he meant was that humour is one of the great signs of the power of the human spirit to overcome tragedy and defeat despair. What we can laugh at, we can survive. Humour is the first cousin of hope.

So it's not surprising that groups who have suffered most often tell the best jokes. I used to love the Jewish comedian Jackie Mason who began his act with the words, 'I may start slowly but little by little I die out completely.' Or Woody Allen's famous line. 'I'm not afraid of dying. I just don't want to be there when it happens.'

The Talmud tells a story about how the prophet Elijah one day came down to earth and showed one of the rabbis two people destined for special reward in the world to come. The rabbi went up to them and asked them what they did. 'We're jesters,' they said. 'When we see someone sad we cheer them up. We turn tears into smiles.' That's what you did for us, Spike, and may you share that reward.

THE COURAGE TO LIVE WITH UNCERTAINTY

1 October 2001

This evening, we begin the Jewish festival of Sukkot, known in English as Tabernacles. It's a simple festival. We take a palm branch, a citron, and some leaves of myrtle and willow to remind ourselves of nature's powers of survival during the coming dark days of winter. And we sit in a *sukkah*, the tabernacle itself, which is just a shed, a shack, open to the sky, with just a covering of leaves for a roof. It's our annual reminder of how vulnerable life is, how exposed to the elements. And yet we call Sukkot our festival of joy, because sitting there in the cold and the wind, we remember that above us and around us are the sheltering arms of the divine presence. If I were to summarize the message of Sukkot I'd say it's a tutorial in how to live with insecurity and still celebrate life.

And living with insecurity is where we're at right now. In these uncertain days, people have been cancelling flights, delaying holidays, deciding not to go to theatres and public places. The physical damage of September 11 may be over; but the emotional damage will continue for months, maybe years, to come. Yesterday a newspaper columnist wrote that looking back, future historians will call ours 'the age of anxiety'. How do you live with the fear terror creates?

For our family, it's brought back memories of just over ten years ago. We'd gone to live in Israel for a while before I became Chief Rabbi, to breathe in the inspiration of the holy land and find peace. Instead we found ourselves in the middle of the Gulf War. Thirty-nine times we had to put on our gas masks and take shelter in a sealed room as SCUD missiles rained down. And as the sirens sounded we never knew whether the next missile would contain chemical or biological warheads or whether it would hit us. It should have been a terrifying time, and it was. But my goodness, it taught me something. I never knew before just how much I loved my wife, and our children. I stopped living for the future and started thanking God for each day.

And that's when I learned the meaning of Tabernacles and its message for our time. Life can be full of risk and yet still be a blessing. Faith doesn't mean living with certainty. Faith is the courage to live with uncertainty, knowing that God is with us on that tough but necessary journey to a world that honours life and treasures peace.

FORGIVENESS

1 October 2003

At this time of the year I can almost feel the approach of Judaism's holiest day, Yom Kippur, the Day of Atonement, which begins this coming Sunday night. It's a day we spend in fasting and prayer, pouring out our hearts to God, saying sorry for the wrong we've done and asking him to grant atonement. A solemn time, though there can be some unintentionally amusing moments.

I remember one year when a synagogue was so oversubscribed that it arranged to have an overflow service in a local cinema. When the day was over and the congregation was leaving, they looked back to see what was playing that week. It turned out to be a film called *Unforgiven*. I hope they had better luck the next year.

But forgiveness is too important to be confined to places of worship. It's the single most important word in conflict resolution. What does it mean? It isn't a substitute for justice. Saying sorry on its own doesn't right a wrong. Nor does it mean forgetting, because we should never forget the past if we want to avoid repeating our mistakes in the future. What it means is drawing a line over the past, saying goodbye to lingering resentments and beginning again. It's one of the most blessed gifts the Bible ever gave humanity.

Think of how many relationships fail because one of the parties doesn't know how to apologize or accept an apology. And what applies to individuals applies to nations and religions. There's a most remarkable group who've been working together in the Middle East for the past eight years – Israeli and Palestinian parents who've lost children in the current conflict. If anyone has a right to be bitter, they have. And yet their grief has brought them together rather than driven them apart. Not because they think peace is easy, but because, having paid so high a price, they don't want others to have to pay it. And so they go round to schools speaking of the need for reconciliation. That takes courage of a high order; but in dark days they've lit a flickering flame of hope.

There was once a man lost in a forest, when he heard the sound of someone approaching. The stranger came up to him and said, 'Friend, I cannot give you directions, for I, too, am lost. But don't take the way I've come from for it too leads nowhere. And now,' he said, 'let's search for a new way together.' Forgiveness means searching for a new way together, and sometimes it's the only way.

TAKING THE LEAP

28 February 2000

If you've taken a look at your calendar recently you've probably remembered that tomorrow is Leap Year Day, the day on which, by old British custom, women are empowered to propose to men. It all began, apparently, in 1288 with that unlikely feminist Queen Margaret of Scotland. It was she who ruled that one day in every four years, on 29 February, any woman could ask for the hand of any man in marriage and, unless he was already married or betrothed, he had either to accept or pay a heavy fine. And maybe it's a custom worth reviving, given the current decline in marriage, and the reluctance men seem to have nowadays to what's become known as the 'C' word: commitment.

I say this because of a really odd experience I had the other week when I helped launch something called National Marriage Week. There I was extolling the virtues of marriage when an interviewer asked me, 'Isn't that very politically incorrect? Who really believes in marriage any more?' To which I had to answer, 'I do, because in this buy it, use it and throw it away society of ours, is there anything more lasting or more gracious than the commitment to share your life with the person you love, and, through that commitment, to bring new life into the world?'

Marriage, sanctified by the bond of fidelity, is the nearest life gets to a work of art. It's what I call *the poetry of the everyday*. And though the moral fashions of today, like yesterday's papers, will one day crumble into dust, of this I am sure: marriage will still be there as the greatest redemption of our loneliness, the point where soul meets soul and we know we are not alone.

And yesterday as I stood under the bridal canopy, officiating at the wedding of a couple we've come to know, I felt again the sheer beauty of that lovely Jewish ceremony, 2,000 years old and yet still fresh, and I thought that maybe that's why Judaism survived – because we always did cherish marriage, the family and the home.

And yes, sometimes it doesn't work out; and I know relationships do fail; but still, surely, there are few risks more worth taking, because where there is peace between husband and wife, you can take all the curve-balls life has to throw at you, knowing you are there for one another in the tough times as well as the good. And it all comes from the 'C' word – commitment – the best investment any of us can make in our future. So for all of you who thought of asking the question but never quite got round to it, remember that tomorrow's a great day for doing so, and I just hope the answer's yes.

THE AGE OF INSECURITY

20 September 2002

Tonight we begin the Jewish festival of Sukkot, Tabernacles. For eight days we leave the comfort of our homes and live in huts, sheds or shacks, with only a canopy of leaves for a roof. It's our way of remembering the forty years during which the Israelites wandered in the wilderness in the days of Moses, without houses or homes; vulnerable to the elements and always ready to move on. It's an ancient festival; and yet I think of it as a festival for our time.

The twenty-first century is, and will remain, the Age of Insecurity. Rarely have we known less what tomorrow will bring. The end of the Cold War brought not peace but a series of intractable local conflicts. Our sense of the safety of everyday life was shaken by 9/11 and left us with a campaign against terror in which we're not always sure who or where our enemies are, and when, if ever, it's succeeded. Meanwhile, our world is changing almost faster than we can bear. And while every previous generation had resources on which to draw at times of change – a job for life, a marriage for life, and a place for life – these, too, have become hard to find. How do you live with insecurity?

That's one thing Jews knew more than most. For almost 2,000 years – exiled, dispersed, scattered throughout the world – they rarely knew whether next year they'd still be there or forced to go somewhere else. As I trace the history of my own ancestors I think of their journeys from country to country, driven by the shifting winds of prejudice and persecution. For them insecurity was a way of life. And its symbol was the *sukkah*, the temporary dwelling with its roof of leaves; exposed to the rain, the wind and the cold.

And what I find moving almost beyond words is that they called this festival of insecurity, *zeman simchatenu*, the season of our joy. What they meant was that we can face anything so long as we know we are not alone. I will fear no evil, because you are with me. Protected by no more than a sense of the divine presence, our ancestors lived through tough times, their sense of humour intact, their appetite for life undiminished. And that, I think, is the message of Sukkot for our time. Faith isn't certainty. It's the courage to live and even celebrate in the very heart of uncertainty, knowing that God is with us, giving us the strength to meet any challenge that undiscovered country called tomorrow may bring.

THE WORLD WE BUILD TOMORROW

21 March 2003

So the armed conflict in Iraq is under way. We've seen the first television pictures of missiles lighting up the night sky. And this morning we've heard of casualties, the British and American troops killed when their helicopter crashed returning from a mission.

At such times, it's almost a natural instinct not just to watch and listen but to want to pray: for those serving in the armed forces and their families; and also for the people of Iraq that they may find the freedom and security to build a better future.

I pray for all the peoples of the region that this moment be a prelude to a new era of peace and not the first thunder in an ever-widening storm. I pray for us in Britain in the coming days and weeks that the real friendship that exists between our different faiths is not strained but strengthened.

Above all I pray for the children of the world, that this time proves a turning point in the history of conflict, as we come face to face with the knowledge of the sheer power we now hold in our hands. Dear God, teach us to use it to dignify life, not destroy it on an unprecedented scale.

But does prayer make a difference? I think it does. It may seem an absurdly fragile thing when set against daisy-cutter bombs, laser-guided missiles and the whole complex technology of modern warfare. And yet I wonder whether it isn't sometimes the strongest thing there is.

Power grows from the barrel of a gun but peace is born in the human heart; and it makes all the difference whether we believe the universe is blind, a place where power rules and only the strongest survive, or whether when we open our hearts, we hear the voice of the creator saying, 'You are all My children, and even your enemies carry the trace of my presence, the mark of my image'?

All the weaponry in the world doesn't add up to the ability to choose between alternative futures. That rests with us, and our faith – expressed in prayer – that the universe is not deaf to our cry, that someone is with us in our fumbling efforts to make the world a little less brutal, a little more humane.

Which is why, in the days ahead, our prayers will make a difference, giving courage to some, comfort to others, and, above all, giving those who live in fear the sustaining power of hope. The world we build tomorrow is born in the prayers we say today.

STAYING YOUNG

22 February 2002

I spend a lot of time these days going around old-age homes, and, to my surprise, they've become one of my favourite places. The residents, usually in their nineties, seem to have an undiminished appetite for life. They joke, argue, complain about the food, and generally have a feistiness that belies their years. I often find myself wishing that I were as young as they are.

I remember meeting a lady in Manchester who was 105. She was in a wheelchair. She said to me, 'I don't want you to think, Chief Rabbi, that I'm usually in a wheelchair. It's just that last night was my 105th birthday party, and we got a little carried away.'

So I've been very struck this week by the debate about the future of the National Health Service and care of the elderly, especially the feeling, on the part of nurses, that they're undervalued. I can't think of any group of people who deserve to be valued more. After each visit to a hospital or an old-age home I come away overwhelmed by the day-to-day kindness and patience of the staff. And I'll never forget how my late father, during the many operations he went through in his eighties, used to say to me, 'I'm not yet in heaven but those nurses are angels.'

Leviticus tells us: 'Stand in the presence of age and honour the face of the old.' And one of the most moving verses in the book of Psalms is the plea: 'Cast us not away when we grow old; as our strength fails, do not forsake us.' I shudder at those who see the elderly as a burden. That must never be. Societies are judged by how they treat the most vulnerable, and that includes the very old.

Many years ago I heard Alastair Cooke tell a story in one of his *Letters from America*. He said that anthropologists had found a remote tribe whose members lived to unusually long old age. A team of researchers was dispatched to discover the cause of their longevity. Was it their diet? Their way of life? The climate? It turned out to be none of these things. What the researchers found was that this was a group who attached great honour to being old. When we value age we help to create it. Which is why we must always show the elderly the care that seeks no return. It may or may not add years to their lives; but it certainly adds life to their years.

PUBLIC OR PRIVATE?

22 November 2002

A story creating debate in America this week is the revelation that Colin Powell decided not to run for election as President because his wife threatened to leave him if he did. She said: 'If you run, I'm gone.' That was back in 1995, when polls showed that he would have won the Republican nomination and defeated Bill Clinton in the presidential race. At the time, all he said in public was that he decided not to run because he lacked the passion and commitment. When he said those words, his wife Alma beamed. Now we know he did it for her.

What a choice to make! Public life or private life? It's one of those ultimate personal decisions for which there are no rules. People in public life are under relentless scrutiny from the media. They have to be prepared for criticism, fair and unfair alike. In some cases there are physical dangers. Mrs Powell believed that as the first black to be elected president, her husband would be at risk of assassination. And of course it's not only those in the limelight who have to pay the price. Sometimes it's harder on their families than on them. So I admire husbands and wives who make sacrifices for their spouses' career. But I respect no less those who make sacrifices in their career for the sake of their wives or husbands.

And there's a detail in Judaism that could almost be a commentary on Colin Powell's decision. In a week's time we'll be celebrating Hanukkah, the Jewish festival of lights. Hanukkah commemorates one of the greatest victories in Jewish history, when, over 2,000 years ago, a small group of Jews overcame the Syrian army of the Alexandrian empire and won back their religious freedom. Remembering that time, we light candles for eight days.

But what do you do, asked the rabbis, if you find yourself on Friday afternoon with only one candle? Do you light it for Hanukkah or for the Sabbath, which also begins with lighting candles? Their answer was simple. You use it as a Sabbath light, not a Hanukkah one. The reason they gave was that the Sabbath candle symbolizes *shalom bayit*, peace in the home. And peace in the home – between husband and wife, parents and children – takes precedence over even the greatest victory in war.

So I salute Colin Powell, who valued marriage more than ambition, his wife more than his career, reminding us that the private light of family burns no less brightly than the public light of fame.

MAKING PEACE

24 September 2001

As we approach the Day of Atonement, the holiest day of the Jewish year, the events in America and Afghanistan still weigh heavily on our minds. We've gone through the stages of a bereavement – first shock, then disbelief, then anger, and now a deep sadness – for the thousands who died, and for a sense of security that has died also. And that will require, not only a diplomatic and military response, but a religious one as well.

Already we've seen the power of religion to express grief, bring comfort, and give hope. There were reports yesterday that in Britain and America, synagogues, churches and other places of worship have been fuller than usual as people seek the company of others and the prayers through which to express their thoughts.

But we've also seen the other face of faith, in the anger of those who committed these terrible deeds, apparently in the name of God. That has nothing to do with Islam, an ancient and honourable faith. It has everything to do with a certain mindset, to which any faith is vulnerable, that seeks to simplify the complexities of life. Religious fundamentalism is the attempt to impose a single truth on a plural world. And that can be deadly.

As a religious believer I have to face the fact that religion is not always a good thing. Usually it speaks to the best in us, but it can sometimes speak to the worst. Religion is like fire. It warms but it also burns. And we are the guardians of the flame.

The great faiths today face their deepest challenge since the wars of religion in the sixteenth and seventeenth centuries. Can the prophetic vision of peace prove stronger than the call to holy war?

One thing is sure: if religion is not part of a solution, it will surely be part of the problem.

Yesterday, the Pope, during his visit to Kazakhstan, spoke of the logic of love that could resolve conflict between the great faiths. And there's another idea, taken from the Day of Atonement: the logic of forgiveness. God, said the sages, forgives us for our sins against Him. But He does not, cannot, forgive us for our sins against people until they, too, have forgiven us. We can only make peace with God when we make peace with our fellow human beings. That's the great antidote to fundamentalism. God has given us many faiths but only one world in which to learn to live together. And in this global age, it's getting smaller all the time.

THE VIEW FROM SPACE

24 September 2003

Did you see those stunning pictures sent back by spaceship Galileo before it crashed two days ago into Jupiter's atmosphere? There they were: crystal clear images of Jupiter's rings and its various moons three billion miles away, one of which, covered in ice, may contain some form of life. And it made me wonder what life on earth looks like from that far away.

It's the great paradox. On the one hand, the whole planet Earth is one tiny point in a universe eighteen billion light years across, and we, so small, so short lived, are mere dust on the surface of eternity. But on the other, what miracles of achievement we're capable of. After all, it's only 100 years since Wilbur and Orville Wright made the first powered flight and now we're sending probes into deep space.

We are so insignificantly small, and yet we remain the only form of life in the known universe capable of asking why we are here. It was all said so precisely in the book of Psalms 3,000 years ago: 'When I look at your heavens, the work of your fingers, the moon and stars you have set in place: what is man that you are mindful of him, the son of man that you care for him? Yet you made him little lower than the angels and crowned him with glory and honour.' We are small, but we have immortal longings, and that's the theme of Rosh Hashanah, the Jewish New Year, which begins this Friday night.

Our other festivals recall great moments in Jewish history, but the new year is our annual celebration of creation, the big bang in which order emerged from chaos, giving rise to stars and planets and life and us. It's the time when we're most conscious of standing in the presence of infinity, as if we were up there with spaceship Galileo looking down on Earth.

And it's hard not to hear a whisper from the soul of the universe that we call God saying, 'Your planet is so small, your life so short, why do you waste so much in conflict and strife, inflicting misery on one another, sometimes even in my name? From down there, the things over which you fight may seem large. From up here they look very small indeed.' Perhaps it's not a bad idea once a year to celebrate the universe and learn to enjoy, not destroy. May it be a good year for all of us and for the world we hold in trust from God.

BETWEEN JUSTICE AND REVENGE

25 June 2001

Until two days ago I never fully understood that strange biblical law of the cities of refuge but now I think I do. The bible has a unique horror of murder because, when it said that each of us is God's image, it gave human life a dignity still unsurpassed. Whoever destroys a single human life destroys an entire world.

And yet, not every act of killing is culpable to the same degree. There are cases where full intent or responsibility were lacking, which is why the cities of refuge were created. They were there to provide a safe haven for people whom the courts had decided did not warrant the full penalty of the law; they protected them from revenge. So long as the killers stayed within the city they were safe, defended by the law from those who felt the law wasn't tough enough.

All of this suddenly became clear to me in the outcry over the release of the killers of Jamie Bulger. That crime was uniquely terrible, a two-year-old child abducted and brutally murdered by two ten-year-old children. I can still remember the wave of revulsion that went through the country, and it was a feeling I shared. And when the killers were convicted there was a disagreement between the home secretary and a senior judge as to how long they should serve. They'd committed a horrendous crime; but they were also ten years old, not yet at the age of full personal responsibility.

Well, they've served their allotted time; and now a new factor has entered the equation, the possibility of revenge from someone who feels that the law has been too lenient. So a huge secrecy operation has had to be put in place to guard them as far as possible from being identified. We've had to reinvent something like, though nowhere near as safe as, that ancient institution, the cities of refuge.

What the Bible was telling us was: never to confuse justice and revenge. It's easy to confuse the two. They are both ways of paying back the criminal for his crime. But between them is a significant difference, the difference called law. It's one thing for society, through the courts, to punish a wrongdoer. It's quite another thing for individuals to take the law into their own hands. Justice sustains the rule of law; vengeance pulls it apart. Which is why, whatever our feelings about Jamie's killers, they must now be safe from revenge. Justice redeems evil. Vengeance merely doubles it.

RUNNING TO STAND STILL

25 September 2000

I was in New York a few weeks ago for a gathering of world religious leaders at the United Nations. As you can imagine, there were an awful lot of speeches, so I confess that while I was there I sneaked out for a few minutes of fresh air in Central Park. And it was there that I saw an extraordinary sight.

New Yorkers tend to be health fiends, and there are always lots of them out in the park, having a jog. One of them, though, obviously didn't want to miss a minute from business, so he was wearing a hands-free mobile phone, into which he was talking, trying to tie up a deal. There he was, running, arguing, negotiating and gesticulating wildly. It was the first time I've seen someone trying to keep fit and risking a heart attack all at the same time.

And then I suddenly thought: what a symbol of our age. Ours was supposed to be the era of leisure; but instead, many of us find ourselves working longer, harder and faster than ever before to earn enough to build a home we're too busy to enjoy, a marriage we're too harassed to celebrate, and children we're too rushed to listen to. We can sometimes be so busy making a living that we hardly have time to live.

Which is why, as a Jew, I feel the need for those High Holy Days – Rosh Hashanah and Yom Kippur – which, in a few days time, will mark the Jewish New Year. The question God asks us on these days is: how have we used our time in the past year? What did we do with that most precious gift of all: the gift of life? There are all sorts of inequalities in the world, but there's one thing we all have equally, and that's time itself. Whether we're rich or poor, there are still only twenty-four hours in the day; 365 days in the year; and a span of life that's all too short.

What I learned after a lifetime of comforting mourners is that what lives on after us is the difference we make in other people's lives. A call to someone who's lonely; a visit to someone who's ill; a listening ear to a person in crisis; time for the members of our family. Those are the things people never forget – not how many phone calls we made while jogging. I don't think anyone's dying words were ever: I wish I'd spent more time in the office. The message of the Jewish New Year is that time is God's gift; let's use it to do one good deed a day.

DANCING WITH THE PAST

26 June 2000

I've just come back from a visit to the Jewish community in Manchester, and one of the things we did yesterday – something we seem to do quite often nowadays – was to consecrate a new *Sefer Torah*, a new scroll of the law. It was a marvellous occasion. It always is. We danced through the streets, taking it in turns to carry the scroll under a bridal canopy, with something of the same exhilaration as King David had, 3,000 years ago, when he brought the holy ark to Jerusalem.

And I was struck, as I am so often, by the strange contrasts in Jewish life. Ours is a pretty forward-looking faith. We welcome scientific and technological advance. Jewish law was quick to embrace *in vitro* fertilization as a blessing to couples who might otherwise be childless; as we will to genetic engineering as a means of curing hereditary disease. Religious Jews are among the most enthusiastic users of the Internet for educational purposes; and in Israel, a country of only five million people, Jews have created the largest high-tech industry outside the United States.

And yet, when it comes to the Torah, the books of Moses from Genesis to Deuteronomy, we still write them exactly as our ancestors have done for thousands of years, by hand, on parchment, using a quill; so that a manuscript written today is almost exactly like the Dead Sea Scrolls, which go back to a time before the birth of Christianity.

There's a view – I hear it in the media almost every day – that in an age like ours, of unprecedented change, our values, too, must change. Forget marriage and the stable family; forget virtues like honour, fidelity, civility, restraint; above all, forget religion. They're old; they're past their sell-by date. For heaven's sake, aren't we living in the twenty-first century?

It's a view that couldn't be more wrong. It's when the winds blow hardest that you need the deepest roots. When you're entering uncharted territory, it's then that you need a compass to give you a sense of direction. What gives us the strength to cope with change are the things that don't change – a loving family, a supportive community, and the religious texts that preserve the wisdom of the past.

And as I carried the Torah scroll through the Manchester streets, I knew beyond the flicker of a doubt that those who carry with them the heritage of the past are those who can face the future without fear.

TAKING THOUGHT FOR THE DAY

26 March 2001

The other day I was phoned up by a gentleman who wanted to know what I thought about the *Today* programme. He's writing the official history and he wanted to know my views. Well what could I say except that I can't think of a better way of being woken up on a Monday morning than by the gracious tones of a Sue McGregor or the good-natured bolshiness of a John Humphrys or a James Naughtie? I'm a fan, and have been since the days of Jack Demanio, who always got the time wrong, and the late Brian Redhead, one of the greatest masters radio ever had.

And then he wanted to know what I thought about *Thought for the Day*. 'Isn't it a bit odd,' he said, 'to have a kind of mini-sermon in the middle of a news programme?' 'Totally,' I said. 'It's wacky, eccentric and wholly benign – exactly like everything else that's great in British culture. There's nothing odder than the British constitution, and yet for centuries, it's been the world's living tutorial in how to create a free society. There's nothing odder than the shape of a London taxi, or the giant ferris wheel called the London Eye, but we love them both and wouldn't have them any other way. Odd is what gives character to a country.'

And then I got serious, because *Thought for the Day* does do two things that are very serious indeed. Firstly, it's made an enormous contribution to our multi-faith society. When I speak in a synagogue, I'm talking to people like me. But right now I'm talking to an audience, most of whom aren't Jewish; and that means I have to speak in a way that spans differences and communicates across boundaries. That's a habit we all have to learn if we're going to be true to ourselves and yet make space for the people who aren't like us. That's what *Thought for the Day* forces people like me to do, and Britain is better because of it.

Secondly, it reminds us that there is something beyond the news. It's called perspective. The news is about today. But the great faiths remind us of yesterday and tomorrow. They're our living dialogue with the past and the future; those two essential things called memory and hope. There's nothing more guaranteed to make us make the wrong decisions than to live solely in the present, forgetting the lessons of the past and our duty to generations not yet born. So, in a world of soundbites and ever-decreasing attention spans, it doesn't hurt to have a daily reminder of eternity. That, at any rate, is my thought for the day.

THE RIGHT TO BE DIFFERENT

26 November 2001

For the next few days Parliament will be debating emergency leg-islation to ban human reproductive cloning. It's happened because a high court judge recently ruled that it isn't covered by existing legislation. And it's become urgent because an Italian doctor has already gone ahead with cloning – to the condemnation of the medical profession.

What is reproductive cloning, and why is it wrong?

It's the attempt to do for humans what Dr Ian Wilmut and his team did in the case of Dolly the sheep. You take a normal cell, isolate its genetic material, insert it into an egg from which the nucleus has been removed, get it to divide like a normal embryo, and then implant it into the womb of a surrogate mother. If it works, the result will be a child who, instead of being a mix of the genes of two parents, will be genetically identical to a single adult. It could be the identical twin of its father. Or it could, I suppose, be a clone of anyone else willing to donate their DNA: Julia Roberts, Dave Beckham, or the actor who plays Harry Potter. It's a new twist to the phrase 'designer genes'.

So what, you might ask, is wrong with that?

Well, the procedure is untried, untested and unsafe. In the case of the experiment that produced Dolly the sheep, 277 eggs were cloned, only twenty-nine developed into embryos, and only one survived to birth. Worse than that – cloned mice have been found to develop subsequent genetic abnormalities that went undetected at birth. Not only is cloning unsafe now; there are good scientific reasons to believe it always will be. So – don't play Russian roulette with a child's life.

But there's a more serious point. What makes us human is the fact that we were conceived, not designed. Because every child is a new combination of two people's genes, it is like, yet unlike, its parents. It has the space to be itself, not what its parents decide it should be. Two thousand years ago the rabbis put it best. They said, 'When a human being makes many coins in a single mint, they all come out the same. God makes every human being in the same image, His image, yet they all come out different.' The glory of creation is that unity in Heaven creates diversity down here on Earth. God wants every human life to be unique. Every child has the right to be a complete surprise to its parents – which means the right to be no one else's clone.

THE VICTORY THAT LASTS

29 November 2002 [Not delivered]

Tonight and for the next seven nights, if you see a house with lighted candles in the window or you drive past a giant candelabrum, that's because we're celebrating Hanukkah, the Jewish festival of lights. And I can't help feeling that it has a message for our time.

Hanukkah recalls the time, more than 2,000 years ago, when the Syrian Greeks tried forcibly to Hellenize the Jews of the land of Israel. They banned the public practice of Judaism and killed those who defied it. A statue of Zeus was erected in the holy temple in Jerusalem. The Jews fought back. They were outnumbered but eventually they won. They recovered their freedom; and rededicated the temple. It was one of the greatest military victories in the ancient world. The thing was, though, that the military victory didn't last. Two hundred and thirty years later a new empire appeared, this time Roman, and the Romans didn't desecrate the temple; they destroyed it completely. Hanukkah, even the Jewish people itself, might have disappeared were it not for one thing. Jews remembered a tiny detail of the story, about how, when they were reconsecrating the temple, they found one cruse of oil undefiled. A miracle happened and it burned for eight days, not one, until new oil could be brought; which is why we light Hanukkah lights as a reminder of those days and a symbol of the eternal light of the human spirit. The military victory lasted until the first century; the spiritual victory, the survival of Jewish faith, has lasted to this day.

We've heard much since 9/11 about the military response to terror: first Afghanistan, now the weapons inspection and possibility of war in Iraq, and after that, who knows? But what about the spiritual response? We know what we're fighting against. Do we know what we're fighting for? On that, the West has been strangely silent. But the fact is – and Hanukkah is the proof – that military victories alone don't last. The big battles grab the headlines. But it's the little battle, the light we light in our homes and hearts, that changes the world because it changes us. The spiritual battle for the sanctity of life against terror in the name of God has hardly yet begun. Hanukkah is about the freedom to be true to what we believe without denying the freedom of those who believe otherwise. It's about lighting our candle, while not being threatened by or threatening anyone else's candle. In this dark world that's the light we need right now.

TERROR IN MOMBASSA

29 November 2002

Mombassa. The latest chapter in the chronicle of terror that's becoming the nightmare of the twenty-first century. Fifteen dead, among them two brothers aged twelve and thirteen; their mother and sister among the eighty injured. It might have been so much worse had the two heat-seeking missiles hit the plane with its 261 passengers instead of missing it by metres. Where does it end, this story that began with 9/11 and has moved from New York to Moscow to Bali and now to the ironically named Paradise Hotel? Not paradise lost but paradise destroyed; knowingly, brutally. How do you fight terror that can be organized anywhere, strike anywhere, take innocent office workers, theatre goers and holiday makers as its victims; that seems to have no logic except hate and rage?

The targets of yesterday's suicide bombing were Israelis about to celebrate the festival of Hanukkah that begins tonight. And perhaps Hanukkah itself has part of the answer. It recalls the moment, almost 2,200 years ago, when the Syrian ruler of the Alexandrian empire, Antiochus IV, tried to impose Hellenism on Israel. He banned the public practise of Judaism and erected a statue of Zeus in the temple. He had power and used it to deny Jews the freedom to live their faith.

The Jews fought back and, though they were outnumbered, they won. They recovered their independence and rededicated the temple. But, oddly enough, on Hanukkah our celebration isn't focused on the military victory. We did not even include the book that tells the story, the book of Maccabees, in the Hebrew Bible. Instead we light candles for eight days, recalling the one cruse of oil found undefiled by those who entered Jerusalem after the war. And for all these centuries, we've recalled at this time the words of the prophet Zechariah: 'Not by might nor by strength but by my spirit says the Lord.'

You can see religion as a battle, a holy war, in which you win a victory for your faith by force or fear. Or you can see it as a candle you light to drive away some of the darkness of the world. The difference is that the first sees other religions as the enemy. The second sees them as other candles, not threatening mine, but adding to the light we share. What Jews remembered from that victory over the Greeks twenty-two centuries ago was not a God of war but the God of light. And it's only the God of light who can defeat the darkness in the human soul.

HANDING ON OUR HOPES

2 April 2001

Three thousand, three hundred years ago, a group of slaves were liberated and began what Nelson Mandela calls 'the long walk to freedom'. And ever since, at this time of the year, we've relived their story on what we call Pesach, Passover, the Jewish festival of the exodus; and we'll be celebrating it soon, at the beginning of next week.

To me, it raises a fascinating question. Imagine we could travel back in time and meet the great Pharaoh himself, Ramses II. I know what I'd say. Ramses, there's good news and bad news. The good news is that one people alive now will be still be alive in thousands of years' time. The bad news is: it won't be yours. It will be that group of slaves out there, building your great temples, the people you call the *habiru* or Hebrews, the children of Israel.

Nothing could sound more absurd. The Egypt of the pharaohs was the greatest empire of the ancient world; and the Hebrews were nothing – slave labour, powerless, not even yet a nation. Yet it was they, not the pharaohs, who survived, and still do to this day. How did it happen? The answer, I believe, is this.

Ancient Egypt and ancient Israel were two peoples who asked the most fateful question of all. How, in this all too brief span of years, do we create something that will endure? How do we acquire a share in immortality? The Egyptians gave one answer: build great monuments of stone – temples, pyramids – that will outlast the winds and sands of time. And they did. What they built still stands. But only the buildings, not the civilization that once gave them life.

The Israelites gave a different answer. You don't need to create monuments. All you need to do is tell the story, generation after generation. You need to engrave your values on the hearts of your children, and they on theirs, so that you live on in them, and so on to the end of time. You need to build a civilization around the home, the school and education as a conversation between the generations. You need to put children first. That is what Jews did for thousands of years; and it's why we're here today.

And if there's one message I would like to shout from the rooftops, it would be this: care about marriage, parenthood and the family. Let's spend time with our children, telling them our story, handing on to them our hopes and dreams. We don't do it enough nowadays; and it makes all the difference. It's the thing, the only thing, that keeps a civilization alive.

THE FAITH CALLED MARRIAGE

8 February 2002

Congratulations to Fred and Olive Hodges, Britain's longest-married couple, who've celebrated seventy-seven years of being together. And in a few hours time, along with Cardinal Murphy O'Connor and others, I'll be helping to launch National Marriage Week. Whatever we feel about today's argument about arranged marriages, once in a while marriage itself deserves a moment of celebration.

What makes it one of the greatest of all human institutions is that it brings together what contemporary life seems so often to split apart – sex, love, companionship, fidelity – and makes of them something greater than the sum of their parts. And far from being outmoded, it seems to me to be made for the twenty-first century.

Why? Because our world is changing almost faster than we can bear. The things that once gave our ancestors a sense of stability – a job for life, a place where we belonged, a set of values that seemed engraved in stone – are all gone. Where then will we find the love that lasts, the knowledge that we matter unconditionally to someone else, something that endures? Not, surely, in relationships that come and go, that we change as often as our car or our television set. They are not the solution; they're the problem.

Elaine and I were married thirty-one years ago, when she was twenty-one and I was twenty-two. In those days we didn't have a clue what life would bring. I hadn't thought of becoming a rabbi, and those early years were full of twists and turns, blind alleys and unexpected avenues. What made the difference for both of us was knowing that the other would be there, that when things were tough neither of us would walk away, that whatever we faced we would not face alone.

Biblical Hebrew has a word for that kind of commitment. It calls it *emunah*, wrongly translated as faith because what it really means is faithfulness, pledging yourself to someone else in the love that is loyalty and the loyalty that's love. That's what marriage is, and I find it moving that the great prophets like Hosea and Isaiah saw it as the closest metaphor of God's love for us and ours for God.

That's why today I'll add my thanks for the gift of love given and received, the love that grows stronger every year because it's renewed every day, the thing called marriage that weaves two lives together and makes of them a grace none of us can ever make alone.

REPENTANCE

2 September 2002

Whatever happened to repentance? I ask the question because we've just begun the countdown to Judaism's holiest days, Rosh Hashanah, the New Year, which begins tonight, and Yom Kippur, our day of atonement. It's a time when we seek out those we may have wronged, and ask for their forgiveness, so that God, too, can forgive us.

It was the anthropologist Ruth Benedict who pointed out the difference between shame cultures and guilt cultures. In a shame culture, what matters is how other people see you, your image in their eyes. Today ours is a shame culture, which is why we have so many spin doctors, so much concern with public image.

Guilt cultures aren't concerned about appearances. They're about the inner voice of conscience; what we used to call the voice of God. In a guilt culture it doesn't matter how others see us. What matters is that we do the right thing. What counts is not other people's opinion, but whether we are peace with ourselves.

The real trouble with shame cultures is that they're unforgiving. Once you've been disgraced, that's it. There's no way back. So in a shame culture the most important thing is to try and bluff it out. It never happened; or if it did, it wasn't me, and if it was me, it wasn't so bad.

But in guilt cultures there's always a way back, because of repentance and the person called God. God forgives. I think that is the greatest single idea the Hebrew Bible ever brought to the world. It means that however often we stumble, we can always start again. God, by giving us free will, empowered us to make mistakes. He never asked us to be perfect. All He asked was that we try our best, own up to our mistakes when we make them, and try a little harder next time. Once we believe in a forgiving God, then it doesn't matter if other people lose faith in us. It doesn't even matter if we lose faith in ourselves. Because somewhere someone has faith in us; and God never loses that faith.

I'd like to see repentance make a comeback. Think of the difference it would make if politicians, business people – any of us – could simply say, I'm sorry, I got it wrong; instead of having to pretend that we got it right. There would be a lot more honesty in public life, and perhaps in private life also, if we really remembered that, whatever we've done, God helps us to begin again.

NATIONAL FORGIVENESS DAY

30 September 2002

The Evangelical Alliance has designated today as National Forgiveness Day; and it's a lovely idea. It lies behind our own Day of Atonement that we observed a fortnight ago. Of all biblical ideas, forgiveness is the most radical antidote to hate.

I remember the day, back in 1999, when I first sensed its urgency. I was visiting Kosovo at the end of the NATO campaign. You could feel the tension. A few months earlier the Kosovan Albanians had fled for safety. Now it was the other side, the Serbs, who feared for their lives. As I stood in Pristina amid the wreckage of war, I realised that only if the Serbs and Albanians could forgive one another and act so as to be forgiven, would they have a future. If not, they would replay their centuries old hostility to the end of time.

Forgiveness is a religious concept. It comes from the idea of a God who loves us as a parent loves a child. In fact the biblical word for mercy, *rachamim*, comes from the word *rechem* meaning a womb. What it means is that once a wrongdoer has apologised for his act and done all he can to mend the harm, we draw a line over the past and begin again. One of the most magnificent examples is at the end of the book of Genesis where Joseph says to his brothers who once sold him into slavery: You intended to harm me but God has turned your intentions to good. With that one act of forgiveness he puts an end to generations of sibling rivalry.

Forgiveness is the only way to live with the past without being held prisoner by the past. Why then is it so difficult? Because it conflicts with our sense of justice. Wrong has been done to us; therefore we feel that it should be avenged. When that wrong is historic, we feel that loyalty to our people demands it even more. Forgiveness can seem like a betrayal. That is why it is so hard.

Why then is it necessary? Because we have a duty to the future as well as to the past – to our children as well as to our ancestors. Long ago Judaism's sages said that God sought to create the world on the basis of justice alone but He saw that it could not survive. That is why He gave us the ability to forgive. In our private lives, and in conflict zones throughout the world, we need it now.

GEORGE

3 December 2001

As a child of the sixties, my teenage memories are forever set to the music of the Beatles. So I couldn't help feeling a little older and a little lonelier when the news came through about the death of George Harrison. As a matter of fact, we live just round the corner from Abbey Road, and most Saturdays, on my way to the synagogue, I walk across the most famous zebra crossing ever to grace the sleeve of a record cover. And it's been a measure of the staying power of the Beatles' music that even now, more than thirty years since the group broke up, fans still come to be photographed there. And this Saturday they were there in their hundreds, outside the studio where the group recorded their greatest hits, in a vigil to the memory of the most inward and perhaps the most intense of the four.

George was always something of a loner compared to the others. And though most of the attention went to Lennon and McCartney, he could produce some stunning music of his own, from that anticipation of the economics of the eighties, 'Taxman', to 'Something', one of the great ballads of all time. It was George who introduced the group to transcendental meditation, and with it the Indian sitar music that he studied with Ravi Shankar; and that love of eastern spirituality stayed with him over the years. There's something about popular music that defines the mood of an age; and it will always be the Beatles music that captures the innocence of the sixties when all you needed was love, and all we were saying was give peace a chance. The world's grown darker since, but sometimes the clouds part, and when they do I still hear George Harrison singing, 'Here comes the sun.'

I was once in a school watching a teacher get a young class to understand the difference between material possessions and spiritual ones. He wanted them to realize that you can lose the first kind but not the second. He spent the morning getting the children to build a model of a house. Then he put on a tape and taught them a song. Then he did something very dramatic. He got the class to break the model and undo the tape. 'Do we still have the house?' he asked. 'No,' they replied. 'Do we still have the song?' Slowly they realized they still did. Thank you, George, for all the music you gave us. We've lost you. But we still have the song.

PLAIN SPEAKING

3 December 2003

Congratulations to Donald Rumsfeld on winning this year's Plain English Campaign award – for those immortal words, 'As we know, there are known knowns … We also know there are known unknowns; but there are also unknown unknowns, the ones we don't know we don't know.' Not much you can add to that really. It's a bit like the poems of Robert Browning about which it used to be said, there were once two people who could understand them: Robert Browning and God. And now there's only God.

It's easy to laugh at the contortions of politicians trying to avoid a straight answer to a straight question. But there is a serious point behind the Plain English Campaign. Just as we're concerned at the purity of the air we breathe and the water we drink, so we should care about the clarity of the words we speak. Waffle, obfuscation and impenetrable jargon are to communication what global warming is to the earth's atmosphere. Debase language and you erode the very environment of thought.

The opening chapters of the Bible are about the importance of language. God says, 'Let there be' and there was. In the beginning was the word. One of our ancient translations reads the phrase that 'man became a living being,' as man became 'a speaking soul'. And when God wanted to stop people building the tower of Babel he simply confused their speech. It wasn't their technical prowess that failed but their ability to make themselves understood. Just as God made the natural world with words, so we make our social world with words, and when they lose their meaning, so too does much else.

When scientists hide behind technical terminology, or specialists use language only a fellow professional can understand, it's like saying to the rest of us: we know what we're doing even if you don't. When politicians take refuge in clouds of verbiage, it's a way of avoiding accountability for things we have a right to know. It's more than courtesy to speak clearly. People who make decisions that have an effect on our lives have a duty to communicate so that we can know what's at stake. What I admire about the prophets of the Bible is that though they had the most exalted visions, they translated them into plain words whose meaning was unmistakable.

To think straight we must speak clearly. To communicate we must speak simply. And to win trust we must speak honestly. Or in plain English, never believe someone you can't understand.

ABRAHAM'S CHILDREN

3 December 2001 [Not delivered]

In the middle of Jerusalem there's a little street, a pedestrian precinct, full of restaurants and coffee bars. It's one of my favourite spots in the city, and I visit it most times I'm there. On Saturday nights, it's full of young people out for a drink after the Sabbath has ended. And it was there, just after midnight this Saturday that two suicide bombers struck, and then a car bomb, leaving ten people dead and 180 injured. And as Elaine and I were shaking with the news yesterday morning, someone rang to tell us that a bomb had exploded in a bus in Haifa. Another fifteen dead; another forty injured. Why did it happen now? Because American envoy Anthony Zinni is visiting the Middle East, trying to engineer a ceasefire. Those who carried out the attacks were willing to murder, maim and commit suicide rather than contemplate the possibility of peace.

I've supported every peace initiative in the Middle East since the Six-Day War, which happened when I was nineteen. I did so for the simplest of reasons. Regardless of where our sympathies lie, it should be obvious that from peace all sides gain. From war, violence and terror everyone loses. People lose their jobs, their future, their security, their lives. Whatever resolution there is to be had, it can only be reached by negotiation, compromise and the slow building of trust. There is no other way. Nothing was ever gained by terror in the modern world, and those who practise it always end by harming their own side more than their enemies. Terror – the deliberate targeting of innocent victims – is evil, whoever practises it and whoever it is practised against; and if we forget that, there's nothing left worth remembering.

Is there, even now, some source of hope? Perhaps just this, that Jews and Muslims both trace their descent to Abraham, and it was in his day that the first recorded territorial dispute took place in the promised land. It happened between Abraham's shepherds and those of his nephew Lot, and Abraham's words then have lost none of their power now. He turned to Lot and said: 'The whole land is before you. If you go to the left I will go to the right. If you go to the right, I will go to the left. Only let there not be a quarrel between us, for we are brothers.' May those who believe in Abraham's God choose Abraham's way: the way of peace.

EATING AND MEETING

4 December 2000

There it was: a little item at the end of last week's news. A new report shows that only fifteen per cent of Britain's families, less than one in six, sit down to have a meal together. A few years ago, a writer on food, noticing the trend, gave it a name. He wrote about how, instead of the traditional family meal, nowadays people come home at different times, take a pizza out of the freezer, stick it in the microwave, and eat it watching television. He called it serial grazing.

Hardly the stuff of headlines perhaps; but it's still worth thinking about. Recently, two new surveys, one from the University of Essex, another from the Rowntree Foundation, have given yet more evidence of the breakdown of marriage and the effect it has on children. Not always, of course, but significantly often, it leads to depression, eating disorders, drug and alcohol abuse, unemployment, violence and crime. And yes, of course, many single parent families are great; and yes, many children from broken or temporary homes grow up just fine. But listen to this comment of a thirteen-year-old girl reported in one of the papers over the weekend: 'I'd like to have a wedding,' she said, 'but not actually marry him. They'll always cheat on you, and then you get hurt.' And when I read that, I thought, what kind of a world have we given her and her contemporaries, in which love, loyalty, fidelity, stability, and the willingness to make sacrifices for one another simply don't exist. She'll be OK. She's already learned to cope. But what we've given her is a narrower, emotionally impoverished world.

And what's that got to do with eating together? Just this: that there are many theories as to why so many marriages fail, or don't even get started in the first place. Some blame it on our material-ist culture; some accuse television and the media; and others point in the direction of poverty and social breakdown. But perhaps at least part of the explanation is altogether more simple. We don't give families time. Time to sit together, eat together, be in one another's company, sharing our problems, our frustrations, our hopes, the simple things that turn a stable family, at its best, into the poetry of everyday life.

And perhaps it's no accident that so many religions place at the heart of their ritual the practice of a shared meal. There is a wisdom there that we shouldn't lose. Eating together means spending time together, and time is the greatest gift we can bring to those we love.

DOING OUR SHARE

4 June 2003

Fat people, said yesterday's headline, will have to diet if they want to see the doctor. The proposal being floated is that patients might have to sign contracts with their doctors, committing themselves to lose weight, or cut down on smoking, or take more exercise, and those who fail to do so could lose their right to free care. Uh-oh, I thought, remembering my losing battle to fight the flab. What a crazy idea – to lose the services of your doctor when you need her most.

But then I remembered Moses Maimonides, the greatest rabbi of the middle ages, and one of the outstanding doctors of his time. And the fascinating thing is that he made much the same suggestion more than 800 years ago. He wrote a pioneering work of preventive medicine – with strong and sound advice about diet, exercise, hygiene and sleep. And the odd thing is that he didn't do it as a keep-fit manual but as part of his classic code of religious law. The body is the gift of God, and therefore he held that we have a religious duty to take care of it. One of the commonest mistakes we make, he said, is to lead an unhealthy life and then blame God when we get ill.

Tomorrow night we'll be celebrating the Jewish festival of Shavuot – when we recall the giving of the ten commandments to Moses and the Israelites: the culmination of their seven-week journey from Egypt to Mount Sinai, from slavery to the great moment of revelation – the journey from the rights to the responsibilities of freedom. By giving the Israelites a set of laws, it's as if God was saying: 'I'll protect you, but I need you to do your share. I'll help you, but you have to help me help you.'

The Bible has a name for this kind of partnership. It calls it a covenant, meaning that both parties pledge themselves to one another, each agreeing to keep their side of the commitment. And I've always felt that a covenant is a model not only for our relationship with God, but for relationships in general – with our marriage partners with whom we share a life, with the teachers who care for our children, and yes, with the doctors who look after our health. So perhaps the idea of a covenant between doctors and patients isn't so crazy after all. They help us, but we have to help them help us. So despite the fact that Jewish festivals usually involve eating, this year I'm going to opt for a little less feeding of the body and a bit more of the soul – in the hope that my doctor will continue to see me, or better still, that I won't need to see her.

EDUCATION AND HUMAN DIGNITY

6 December 2002

Two days ago, on my way to a meeting in the centre of London, I found myself in the middle of the student march, part of the continuing argument about university fees. And if I hadn't been due elsewhere, I think I would have joined them.

When I went to university, I was the first member of my family to do so. My late father, who'd come to this country as a refugee, had to leave school at the age of fourteen to help support the family. And one of the things he most wanted for his four boys was that we should have the education he missed. He knew, as did we, that it would open up opportunities for us that he'd been denied; and if it had cost very much, we probably wouldn't have had that chance.

Education has been a Jewish passion since the start. Moses said, in what's become our most famous prayer, 'You shall teach these things diligently to your children.' Ezra, leading the exiles back from Babylon, instituted one of the first great programmes of adult education. And by the first century, 1800 years before England, the Jewish people had a system of compulsory universal education, paid for from public funds. Where other nations built castles, Jews built schools and academies. It's not too much to say that that's how we survived.

I wonder if, to this day, we realize what a radical vision lies at the heart of the Hebrew Bible. Throughout history, there have been two great attempts to shape a society of equal dignity. The first has been to try and create a situation where everyone has equal access to power through the political system. The second focuses on equal access to wealth through the economic system.

The Bible offers a revolutionary alternative: concentrate on equal access to knowledge through the educational system. And it's the only one of the three that really works – because when it comes to power or wealth, the more you share, the less you have. That's why politics and economics always have been, and always will be, arenas of conflict. But when you share knowledge you don't have less. The more you share, the more there is. Which is why the prophet Isaiah said, 'And *all* your children shall be taught of the Lord and great shall be the peace of your children.' More than wealth or power, education is the key to human dignity. That's why, when it comes to the pursuit of knowledge, *all* our children should have an equal chance.

BETWEEN TWO EVILS

5 March 2003

As the countdown ticks ever closer to some form of confrontation with Iraq, I've rarely known Britain so divided. Many passionately believe that war is misconceived and morally wrong. It'll cause suffering to the Iraqi people. It will create chaos there and destabilize the Middle East. It will incite anger and give birth to yet more terror.

But there are those who, with no less passion, no less moral principle, are convinced that unless we confront tyranny and terror, not only will we be perpetuating the suffering of the Iraqi people, we'll be storing up, if not for us then for our children; a future in which weapons of mass destruction with global reach are in the hands of those who care nothing for the sanctity of life, and who have no qualms about the mass murder of the innocent.

In such a situation it may seem idiosyncratic to quote some of the opening lines of the Bible, but it's there that we find a remarkable idea usually lost in translation.

It says, 'And God said, Let there be light, and there was light. And God saw that the light was good, and separated the light from the darkness, and called the light "day" and the darkness "night". But then the Bible doesn't go on to say what we would have expected it to say: 'there was day and then night,' or 'there was light and then darkness.' It uses two words we haven't met before: 'And there was *evening* and there was *morning*.' And what we miss in translation is that the Hebrew word for evening, *erev*, means a mixture of light and dark; and the word for morning, *boker*, means breaking through; as the first rays of the sun pierce the shroud of night.

What the Bible is telling us with great subtlety is that for God there may be black and white, but human time is lived in shades of gray, mixtures of light and dark. Which is why the great fateful decisions are so difficult. Clashes between right and wrong are easy. But often the clash is between two wrongs, neither of which we would choose in an ideal world, but between which, given the world as it is, we must decide.

That's why I pray not only that God give our leaders wisdom in the days that lie ahead, but that He gives us, too, the generosity of spirit to unite in our vision of a safer, more just, less brutal world, even as we differ on how to get there.

THE CRY OF A CHILD

6 September 2002

Tonight sees the beginning of Rosh Hashanah, the Jewish New Year, the beginning of ten days of penitence in which we reflect on the past, rededicate ourselves to the future, and ask God in the coming year to write us in the book of life.

Jewish tradition sees the New Year as the anniversary of creation, the big bang; the moment the universe began. And one thing has always struck me about these days: the biblical readings we recite in the synagogue. You would have thought we would read the majestic opening chapter of the Bible: And God said let there be, and there was. The story of creation.

But actually we don't. Instead, we read about the birth of the first Jewish child, Isaac, born to Abraham and Sarah after many years of waiting. We read about Hannah and her prayer for a child, which was also answered. I find that deeply moving. On this day of days we read not about God's act of creation, but about ours; not about the echoing vastness of the universe, eighteen billion light years across; but about the joy and responsibility of bringing new life into the world. We don't think of God as the master scientist devising systems of organized complexity, but as a parent, loving and forgiving us, his children.

There have been times, these past twelve months, when the problems of the twenty-first century – Afghanistan, Iraq, the Middle East, the environment, the global economy – have seemed almost impossibly intractable. How do you begin to get a grip on issues so difficult to analyse, let alone solve? Yet one thing seems clear to me; that what matters is not only the critical intelligence we bring to bear, but also our fundamental vision, our starting point. And on this the Jewish New Year has something simple but quite important to say. Don't think about the past; or even present calculations of political interest or economic gain. Ask what impact this will have on future generations. Have in front of you the image of a single human child.

Children are the sufferers of the twenty-first century. One hundred and thirteen million of them have no schooling. One hundred and fifty million are malnourished. Thirty thousand die each day from preventable diseases. They have no vote, no power, no voice, yet they are the ones who'll suffer tomorrow for the mistakes we make today. The message of Rosh Hashanah is that greater even than an understanding of creation is the ability to hear the cry of a child.

SCIENCE AS A BLESSING

8 October 2003

What a wonderful story lies behind yesterday's announcement that a British scientist Sir Peter Mansfield has won the Nobel Prize for medicine. Clearly he's one of the world's great scientists but his story holds a message of hope for everyone who didn't do that well at school. Because Sir Peter left school at the age of fifteen with no qualifications and an ambition to become a printer.

In fact he might never have developed an interest in science had it not been for the V2 rockets that fell on London towards the end of the Second World War. That led to an interest in explosives and one thing led to another. So never believe that leaving school with no qualifications means that the doors of the future are closed. Two of the most successful people I've ever met were told by their headmasters that they'd never amount to anything. Once in a while, hope and a focused mind can defeat any setback.

Sir Peter's achievement is hopeful in another way as well. He discovered that the nuclei of atoms have a spin that can be controlled by a magnetic field, and when they return to normal, the energy they've absorbed turns them into tiny radio transmitters. The stroke of genius was to see that this could be used to give continuous pictures of the inside of the human body. It's called magnetic resonance imaging, or, to you and me, an MRI scan. If you've ever had one you'll know what magic it is. It's painless, harmless and produces crystal-clear images. It's a major diagnostic tool, and because it's non-invasive I hope it'll one day replace many post-mortems as well.

This is science at its best, saving lives, and honouring the dignity of the human body. We've become anxious about science and its power to destroy. But for me the greatest truth was signalled long ago. The first chapter of Genesis describing creation begins with the second letter of the Hebrew alphabet; the ten commandments begin with the first: to tell us that even greatest act of creation is secondary to the uses to which we put it. Every technology can be used for good or evil, which is why the greater our scientific knowledge, the stronger must our ethics be.

Sir Peter Mansfield not only discovered MRI but saw how to turn it into a blessing. So let's raise our coffee cups and drink a toast to a man who has been, in that lovely Jewish phrase, a partner with God in the work of creation.

IT TAKES MORE THAN WAR TO MAKE PEACE

29 March 1999

As we witness the unfolding tragedy of Kosovo, Jews throughout the world are getting ready to observe Pesach, Passover, the Jewish festival of freedom which begins this Wednesday night. And I'm struck by the thought of how contemporary this most ancient of religious rituals still is.

It's more than 3,000 years since the exodus took place. And yet ever since, Jewish families have sat together round the table to tell the story of how their ancestors were once slaves, and how they lived under the shadow of attempted genocide. My first memories as a child are of those nights in my grandparent's house, when I first ate the unleavened bread of affliction and the bitter herbs of suffering, and drank four cups of the wine of freedom. It was the simplest and yet the most powerful of history lessons. It taught me, as it teaches every Jewish child, to be ready to face a world that's full of pain and yet never without hope. Already then, not more than three or four years old, I was beginning to understand how wrong it is for one people to deprive another of its liberty; and how tyranny always ultimately defeats those who use it against others, from the Pharaohs to the present day.

One thing has long fascinated me. It's how Moses, on the brink of the exodus, summoned the Israelites and addressed them. He could have spoken about many things – freedom, or the promised land, or the long journey that lay ahead. But he didn't. Instead, three times, he spoke about the distant future, and about the duty of parents to teach their children the story of the going out of Egypt; and we still do. It was the oddest thing to say, but it was also the wisest. Because to defend a country, you need an army. But to defend humanity, you need education. You need parents to teach children the story of freedom, and once a year you need children to taste the bread of affliction so that they learn never to inflict it on others.

I support the NATO intervention in Kosovo and I pray that it succeeds. But when it's over, all the problems will still remain. Serbs and Albanians will still need to live together, each respecting the freedom of the other, each willing to move beyond the hatreds of the past. You can't achieve that by air strikes alone. It can only come from a long, patient effort of education. When will we learn that peace doesn't grow from the barrel of a gun? It's born in the hearts of human beings, and its seeds are planted in the stories we teach our children.

TELL YOUR CHILDREN

31 May 1999

Here's a lovely idea. Last Friday a group called Parentalk launched a new initiative. Its aim? Simply to get parents to say three words to their children. The words 'I love you.' Just that. Tell your children you love them.

Well, what with Kosovo, and Manchester United and the row over Sophie's pictures, it didn't quite make the front page headlines. But I wonder which in the long run will have more of an effect on our lives and the lives of those around us.

One of the privileges of being in public life is that I've come to know people who in one way or another exercise a great deal of power – politicians, heads of businesses, figures in the media and academic life. People spend a lot of time, sometimes whole lives, pursuing that kind of power, perhaps because they feel that if they have it their lives will make a difference. What they do, what they say, will affect others.

And yet, for how long? Leaders come and go, other people take over and do things differently, and the influence anyone has in public life is like a picture drawn on a beach in the sand: clear for a while but only till the tide turns.

And now think about being a parent. Think of the influence we have on our children, or the influence our parents had on us. Is there anything that made more of a difference – not just for a moment but for a lifetime?

Which of us doesn't carry some memory of words our parents said to us when we were young – words that hurt, or words that made us walk tall?

Those are the words we never forget, and they shape our image of who we are. If they hurt, we can spend much of our adult life trying to ease the pain. But if they gave us pride or confidence, it stays with us through the years. Tell your child you love her, you love him, and in that one act of letting them know they are loved, you give them the strength to love in return. I don't know of a greater gift; and all it takes is a few seconds of our time and our heart.

I tell you, not one in a thousand of the people who fill the news has the power that a parent has over his or her child – the power to change a life. And if you find that hard to believe, think of the Bible. The prophets knew that God was mightier than the greatest politician. But when they spoke of His power they did so in one image. He is our parent, we are His children, and the most important thing He ever did for us to communicate His love. So this Bank Holiday, let's take a moment with our children and give them what God gives us.

Postscript:

Years later, I was launching National Marriage Week and the lady introducing me told the following story. She had been listening to me on the radio (it was the talk above) and she decided to do what I suggested. Taking her children to school that morning, she turned to them and said, 'I love you.' Her young daughter, in the seat behind, said: 'Oh Mum, how embarrassing can you get? I bet you've been listening to *Thought for the Day* again.' Which just goes to show, really.

OF ARMIES AND SCHOOLS

7 June 1999

This morning's news of the collapse of talks about Kosovo means that the war will continue, even intensify. So we still wait and pray that somehow an agreement may yet emerge to allow the refugees to return and rebuild their shattered world. The question is: what then?

We now know how hard it is to end the war. But it'll be an even greater challenge to sustain a peace. Suppose, some time this week, an agreement is signed. A peacekeeping force is established. The Kosovar Albanians return. Some semblance of normality prevails. Meanwhile, though, a country has been devastated, homes destroyed and townships ruined. Stories will emerge of terrible atrocities. Even when hostilities end, there'll be a legacy of bitterness on both sides. How do you break the circle of hate?

I know of only one answer. The Bible tells the story of how the Israelites were enslaved in Egypt, and how the Pharaoh, faced with the destruction of his country, kept changing his mind, until Moses finally led his people to freedom. And yet, when it was all over, Moses spoke to the next generation and gave them a remarkable command. 'Don't hate the Egyptians,' he said. Yes, you've been through bad times, but now you must move on. If you spend your time trying to destroy your enemies you will end by destroying yourselves. That is the message that must be heard today by Serbs and Albanians in this tense part of the world. And that needs a massive effort of education.

Listening to the news, we can sometimes think that peace is a matter of military campaigns, diplomatic pressure and negotiated settlements. And so it is, but only in the short term. In the long run, peace depends on other things – learning to coexist, making space for others, letting go of the past and moving on. One of the things I found most moving in this war was the work done by Israeli teenagers who flew to Kosovo to work with traumatized children. They used their own experience among victims of terror to bring healing a long way from home.

Billions of pounds have been spent on this war. Even more will be spent on repairing the damage. What if a mere tenth of that amount were spent on teaching children to see that not only I but also my enemy is capable of suffering and pain? Armies win wars, but it takes education to make peace. Because though war needs physical courage, peace needs moral courage, the courage to break with the past and turn enemies into friends.

KINDERTRANSPORT

14 June 1999

Tomorrow morning I'll be taking part in what I guess is going to be one of the great emotional experiences of my life. More than a thousand people will be coming together to remember the day, sixty years ago, when their lives were saved by an act of kindness on the part of Britain and its citizens. They are some of the people, rescued as children in the operation known as Kindertransport.

Already by November 1938 most people knew that, under the Nazis, Jews were doomed. On a single night, Kristallnacht, 191 synagogues were set on fire and another seventy-six completely demolished. Thirty thousand Jews were rounded up and sent to concentration camps. It was the beginning of the end.

Out of that darkness came one small beacon of light. The British government announced that it was willing to admit 10,000 children from Germany, Austria and Czechoslovakia. It was an act of humanity unmatched anywhere else in the world, and it literally saved their lives. Most of those who stayed were murdered. Many of those who came never saw their families again. And none have ever forgotten that journey, as they waved goodbye to their parents and travelled to the one place that would let them in.

Many of them, including several friends of ours, have devoted their adult lives to the service of others, giving back some of the kindness that was shown to them. Tomorrow they'll be coming to give thanks to the many people in this country who opened their doors, their homes, and their hearts.

And that same British compassion still lives. The head of the Refugee Council told me of something he'd witnessed a week or two ago. He was up in the Midlands, meeting a group of Kosovan refugees, when someone came to tell him that there was a demonstration outside. His heart sank, until he went out and saw what was written on the placards. Just one word. 'Welcome!'

And when those refugees return home, they'll carry with them the memory of that moment – the knowledge that there is another way of treating strangers, not with hostility but hospitality. And who knows if that isn't the best way of healing a fractured world.

Acts of kindness never die. They linger in the memory, giving life to other acts in return. And as the Jewish children of sixty years ago join their thanks with those of the Kosovar Albanians of today, I know that while courage on the field of battle wins wars, it's another kind of courage – the gift of refuge in times of danger – that gives human hope a home.

IN PRAISE OF TEACHERS

21 June 1999

The other day, I was taking part in a seminar, and the response to something I said made me aware that we don't say it enough.

We'd come together – academics, planners and politicians – to discuss the connection between schools and citizenship. Citizenship will become part of the national curriculum in two years time, and we were sharing ideas about how to make it work. In the course of my remarks I happened to say that we don't honour teachers enough. We blame schools when they fail, which is rarely. But we don't sing their praises when they succeed. To my surprise, that got a loud cheer. It was clear that I'd hit on a forgotten truth.

For us as Jews, the greatest leader we ever had was Moses. And what fascinates me is the title we gave him. Moses was a liberator, a law-giver, a military commander and a prophet. But we call him none of these things. Instead we call him *Moshe Rabbenu*, 'Moses our teacher', because that, for us, is the highest honour. And the reason, I think, is this.

Long ago the Jewish people came to the conclusion that to defend a country you need an army. But to defend a civilization you need schools. The single most important social institution is the place where we hand on our values to the next generation – where we tell our children where we've come from, what ideals we fought for, and what we learned on the way. Schools are where we make children our partners in the long and open-ended task of making a more gracious world.

And so, from the biblical era to today, Jews became a people whose passion was education, whose greatest love was learning, whose citadels were schools and whose heroes were teachers.

Jewish law contains an extraordinary provision. In ancient times there were places set aside as cities of refuge for people needing protection. And the rabbis ruled that if a student has to go there, his teacher has to go with him. Why? Because, in their words, *life without a teacher is simply not a life.*

Teachers open our eyes to the world. They give us curiosity and confidence. They teach us to ask questions. They connect us to our past and future. They're the guardians of our social heritage. We have lots of heroes today – sportsmen, supermodels, media personalities. They come, they have their fifteen minutes of fame, and they go. But the influence of good teachers stays with us. They are the people who really shape our life.

THE COURAGE TO FORGIVE

10 September 1999

I've just got back from Kosovo. I went there to see how that troubled region is putting itself back together again after the conflict. And it was there, standing among the bombed buildings and the wreckage, that I suddenly realized the power of one word to change the world – the word 'forgiveness' – the key word for Jews at this time.

Tomorrow and Sunday we celebrate Rosh Hashanah, the Jewish new year; and a week after that, Yom Kippur, the Day of Atonement. And despite their intense solemnity, they're really about something very simple. These are the times when we apologize to God – and to our fellow human beings – for the wrong we've done and the hurt we caused. We ask for forgiveness so that we can begin again. Which is exactly what Serbs and Albanians are going to have to do if there's ever to be peace in that part of the world.

One of the most interesting discoveries in recent years came when a group of biologists solved a problem posed, more than a century ago, by Charles Darwin. What fascinated Darwin was the question of how all human societies come to value altruism. Surely evolution should favour the ruthless, not the good? But actually it turns out the other way.

Using computers, biologists simulated different kinds of human being. Those that flourished were the ones capable of sustaining cooperation. What they also found – and this was the real discovery – was that in the long run you had to include in the programme a system of forgiveness. You have to instruct the computer-generated person periodically to forget the wrongs it suffers. Otherwise it gets locked in a cycle of revenge and retaliation, and everyone loses. Without having a clue what it was doing, the computer was simulating what's actually happened in the Balkans, East Timor, Northern Ireland, and the Middle East. Rarely has science so clearly proved the truth of a great religious idea.

Forgiveness is the most powerful thing the Bible ever taught humanity, and we're going to need it in the years to come. Because what will our grandchildren say of us if we solve all the problems of technology and yet fail to resolve the problem of human conflict. The Jewish new year has a message for us all. Say sorry to those you've hurt and forgive those who've hurt you. Easy? No. But unbelievably powerful. It takes a only little courage to fight; a great deal of courage to forgive. A peaceful new year to you all.

THE LIGHT OF HOME

6 December 1999

Over the next few days, if you pass a house with candles burning in the windows, chances are that it's a Jewish family celebrating Hanukkah, the Jewish festival of lights. It's our way of celebrating a moment in Jewish history about two centuries before the birth of Christianity. Israel was under Greek rule, which began to suppress our religious practices. Jews rose in rebellion and won back their freedom. The Temple was rededicated, and the great *menorah* or candelabrum was relit. And ever since, we too have lit candles to remind us of that time.

Like so many Jewish festivals, it takes place at home – parents and children celebrating together; lighting candles, singing songs – and, well, it wouldn't be Jewish if it didn't have food, which on Hanukkah means donuts and potato pancakes. Judaism isn't a religion of the kitchen, but it's surely a religion of the home.

And that's my thought for the day. For the past few days, following the launch of the National Family and Parenting Institute, there's been a fierce debate about the future of the family, and I suspect it'll carry on long into the new millennium. Is the family – by which I mean father, mother and children linked in a stable bond of love – just a passing phenomenon? Can we do without it? Is it just one lifestyle among many? How do you answer such questions in a way that's more than subjective?

One of the things about being part of an ancient faith is that, however new a problem seems, our ancestors have been there before, and they've passed on their experience to us. At the time of Hanukkah, 2,200 years ago, the Greeks dominated the world. Their power seemed invincible. And Jews – well, they were a tiny people.

And yet within a few years Greece began its decline and fall, yet Jews and Judaism survived; they still do.

What was the difference? The Greeks focused on politics and the state. Jews placed their faith in something smaller – the family and the home. And somehow, in doing so, they hit on a great truth: that when families are strong, children are strong, and they can face the future without fear. When families are weak, children grow up anxious and confused and a civilization begins its decline. The future of our world won't be decided by the Euro, the Internet, or space probes to Mars, but by how much or how little we value our children – by the flame we light at home.

REVERENCE, RESPONSIBILITY, RESTRAINT

20 December 1999

Hardly a week passes these days without news of some breathtaking new scientific discovery – mostly the result of the greatest research project ever – the mapping of the human genome, the decoding of life itself. A few days ago British scientists announced that they'd completed the first stage, the script of chromosome twenty-two, one of the twenty-three that make up the human genetic profile. Then came news that an American team had worked out a formula for creating new life forms in the laboratory.

By any standards this is an extraordinary moment. The nineteenth century was about industrial technology; the twentieth about information technology. But the twenty-first century will be the age of biotechnology; and the questions it'll raise will be formidable.

The good news is very good indeed. There's a real chance that soon, scientists will be able to isolate the causes and find cures for a whole series of genetic disorders like Huntington's disease and cystic fibrosis. They may even discover new ways of treating congenital heart disease and some cancers, such as leukaemia.

But the other possibilities are far more problematic. There's the question of cloning, applied to human beings. There's the prospect that scientists might create transgenic animals or entirely new forms of bacteria and virus. There's even the possibility of designer babies, children born with artificially enhanced genes to make them super-bright or mega-beautiful. For the first time in history, we have the power to change the genetic make-up of life on earth, and the scientist Edward Wilson rightly says that this will present the most profound intellectual and ethical choices humanity has ever faced. How then shall we proceed?

Right at the outset the Bible makes an extraordinary statement. For six days God created. But the day the Bible calls holy is the seventh day, the day God stopped creating. Even for God there are limits; and we now know that the limits within which life can flourish are very fine indeed.

Not everything we can do, should we do. It's one thing to use technology to heal; quite another to make genetic changes that will have incalculable consequences for the future. Life is God's gift, and we are its guardians. So I want to propose a new set of three R's to take us into the next century: *reverence, responsibility* and *restraint*. Never have we needed them more than now.

LETTING GO OF THE PAST

6 October 2000

On Sunday night Jews throughout the world will be in a synagogue for the start of Yom Kippur, our Day of Atonement, the holiest day of the Jewish year. For twenty-five hours we don't eat or drink; we spend the whole day in prayer; and I don't think there's any time when we feel more acutely the presence of God.

But this year we approach the day with a heavy heart, feeling in our very bones the pain of conflict in the land of Israel; the violence and bloodshed which would be tragic at any time, but doubly so now, because they've come as a result, not of war, but the pursuit of peace. Like many on both sides, I feel it personally. Two of my brothers live in Jerusalem. Our daughter is studying there now. And when I stand in the synagogue, I can't help but ask: why is peace so difficult, especially in the land God called His own, and in Jerusalem, the city whose very name means peace?

My own answer, controversial though it may be, is this: peace is hard because, for both sides, it means letting go; letting go of the past, and of our feelings of being wronged. How can we let go of that pain? And yet we must, for the sake of our children and the future, Jewish and Muslim, because otherwise we face an endless cycle of retaliation and revenge. There's only one way to break that cycle, and that's to answer violence with a renewed search for peace.

And that's the meaning of Yom Kippur. It's about breaking the tragic grip of the past. To be human means that we make mistakes, we hurt other people, we inflict pain. But at this time of the year we try to put these things right. We apologize to those we've harmed; we forgive those who've harmed us; we answer God's call to turn enemies into friends. Perhaps the deepest message of the Day of Atonement is that it's never too late to begin again.

And that's what the Middle East needs right now. It needs politicians to engineer a cease fire. But it needs more. It needs the courage of ordinary men and women, Israelis and Palestinians, to let go of the past and begin again, knowing that we can achieve through peace what none of us will ever achieve through violence. There's only one thing more powerful than weapons of destruction, and that's words of forgiveness and reconciliation. I pray to God that we find them now.

LETTING GO OF HATE

23 January 2004

This coming Tuesday I'll be in Belfast for Holocaust Memorial Day. This year we'll remember not just the destruction of two-thirds of European Jewry, but also the devastating tragedy in Rwanda when in the spring of 1994 a brutal conflict claimed the lives of over 800,000 people in the space of a hundred days.

I remember when Holocaust Memorial Day was first announced, on 27 January 2000. I was in Stockholm, where a gathering of more than twenty European heads of state committed themselves to a continuing programme of education in the evils of genocide. At the time, people asked, 'Why do we need to remember? Surely all that was in the past.' Since then we've had 9/11, the wars in Afghanistan and Iraq, repeated acts of terror throughout the world – and who knows what else lies in store in this tense and troubled age.

There is only one cure for the virus of hate, namely education. Two years ago for Holocaust Memorial Day I went to a school in south London. The pupils came from forty-three different language groups – almost every religion and ethnicity you could imagine – and together we listened to two pupils, one Muslim, the other from Africa, speaking about a visit they'd made to Auschwitz, and how it had changed their lives.

Everyone sat in total silence. And when the assembly was over and people were filing out, some of the eleven-year-olds in the front row called me over and said, 'Sir, we want you to know that if anyone picks on someone in this school, we're there to protect them. We don't allow any racism here.' And I thought: if only such moments could be replicated around the world, how much grief we might spare, how many lives we might save in the years to come.

And then I remembered one of the most moving sentences in the Bible, when Moses, just before his death, turns to the children of the next generation and says, 'Don't hate an Egyptian, because you were a stranger in his land.' Don't hate the people who persecuted their parents and made their lives hell? How could he say such a thing? But the truth is: he knew that *to build a society of freedom, you have to let go of hate.* Without that, he might have taken the Israelites out of Egypt, but he would have failed to take Egypt out of the Israelites. That's what Moses taught the children of his time, and it's what we must teach the children of ours.

THE HERO WITHOUT A GRAVE

4 March 2004

Tomorrow night and the following day, we'll be celebrating the festival of Purim. We'll remember the events described in the book of Esther, which records the first warrant for genocide, Haman's decree to 'destroy, slay and exterminate all Jews, young and old, women and children, in one day'. That plan was averted, which is why we celebrate. But it was revived not that long ago, in the Wannsee conference in January 1942, when Germany adopted the so-called 'Final Solution' to the Jewish problem by eliminating all the Jews of Europe.

It's against that background that I'm going this morning to a ceremony to honour the memory of one of the true heroes of the twentieth century, the Swedish diplomat Raoul Wallenberg. Wallenberg was sent, at the age of thirty-two, to be part of the Swedish diplomatic mission in Budapest in July 1944. By then the mass extermination of Hungarian Jews was under way. Over 400,000 of them had already been killed in Auschwitz.

With courage, imagination and a single-minded sense of purpose, he resolved to do what he could to save at least some of those who remained. He printed and handed out Swedish protective passports. He created safe houses where Jews could take refuge. In some cases, he even rescued people who'd already boarded the transportation trains. And he managed to delay Eichmann's planned massacre of Budapest ghetto, so that when the Russians reached the city two days later they found over 90,000 Jews still alive. One way or another he saved more than 100,000 lives.

We don't know what happened to him. Suspected of being an American spy, he was taken to Russia, and there all traces of him disappear. He remains the hero without a grave. But as long as humanity remembers those days, his name will remain a symbol of courage in the face of seemingly invincible evil. He stood firm. He refused to be intimidated. He resisted, knowing that in dark times what we do makes a difference. The good we do lives after us, and it's the greatest thing that does.

Two thousand years ago the sages said, 'A single human life is like a universe.' Save a life, and you save a world. Change a life and you begin to change the world. That was Raoul Wallenberg. And in an age like ours of religious hate and global terror, his message could not be clearer. To love God is to recognize His image in a human face, especially one whose creed, colour or culture is different from ours. May his memory inspire us.

FATHERS

19 March 2004

There was a report in yesterday's papers about some remarks made by the Prince of Wales in sympathy with divorced fathers campaigning for greater access to their children. And today a conference is taking place in Edinburgh to discuss ways in which more positive father–child relationships can be supported.

I vividly remember the morning a few months ago when I got stuck in a traffic jam on my way to do *Thought for the Day* and discovered that what had brought traffic to a standstill was a divorced dad dressed as Father Christmas, protesting what he saw as the injustice done to him over custody rights.

And I must say I was sympathetic to his cause – because children need the chance to develop a relationship with both their natural parents. After all, no child ever asked to be born. That was a responsibility two people took in bringing him or her into being; and neither in any ordinary circumstances should be denied the exercise of parenthood.

The trouble is, of course, that divorce at present is all too common and often very acrimonious. Each side seeks a legal victory over the other and, whoever wins, it's often the children that lose.

Fatherhood itself has become problematic in our culture. I first realized how bad things had become back in the 1980s. I'd been giving a talk about family life to a group of Jews and Christians in the north of England, and a local vicar came up to me afterwards and said, 'I've spent my whole life teaching children about "God the father", but I can't do it any more. They don't understand what I'm talking about. And the word they don't understand isn't "God" but "father".'

It's actually fatherhood that makes humanity different from most primate species. Usually it's the females who look after the young, while a few weeks after birth many males don't even recognize their own children. Motherhood is biological and almost always strong. Fatherhood is cultural and almost always in need of support. In fact, I suspect that's why the Bible so often speaks of God as a father – not because God is male, nor in order to create a patriarchal society, but simply to moralize and dignify paternal responsibility. Like a good father God cares about his children. He protects them, listens to their hopes and fears, and when they turn to Him, He's there.

Which is why we need to support both parents, even when they split apart. Children need time with both – and it's *their* needs that really count.

TERROR IN MADRID

12 March 2004

'How like a widow is the city once great among the nations.' Those words from the Book of Lamentations went through my mind as I heard of yesterday's terrible events in Madrid. And all we can offer the people of Spain is the human solidarity of grief, our voices joined in prayer for healing for the injured, comfort for the bereaved, courage for the survivors, and strength for those still engaged in rescue.

This was an evil deed; devastating in its scope, tragic in its consequences. And I feel all the more emotional having just made a trip to Jerusalem to visit the victims of terror there. Rarely do we see its long-term effects. For a day or two, news of an atrocity fills our screens and then the attention of the media moves elsewhere. But what is left behind are shattered lives: scars, trauma and grief that may never fully heal.

We sat with an eleven-year-old boy who'd lost half his family when a bomb went off in a restaurant; and he himself was now blind. We sat with other children who'd been on their way to school when the bus exploded, killing their friends and changing their world for ever.

That's what makes terror so much worse than war. In war there's a battlefield. In terror; a shop, an office, a train can become a battlefield. In war there are targets. In terror anyone is a target – the innocent, the passers-by, the uninvolved. In war there is a logic. In terror there is no logic, because there never was, nor ever will be, anything achieved by it that could not have been achieved by other means. No responsible government can ever negotiate with terror, because to give in to it is not to end it but to invite yet more.

Terror has no defence. It's born, not of despair, but of contempt. It's destruction for destruction's sake.

And how ironic that this should have taken place in Spain where once, a thousand years ago, Jews, Christians and Muslims lived together more peaceably and creatively than anywhere else in medieval Europe.

Today throughout the world the very soul of liberty is being tested. It's no accident that these bombs went off just days before a general election, because terror is the ultimate enemy of freedom: the attempt not to reason with but to kill those with whom you disagree. Which is why it will always fail. Love of life will always defeat disdain for life. Dear God, may it do so soon.